Beyond *A Love Supreme*

BEYOND *A LOVE SUPREME*

John Coltrane and the Legacy of an Album

Tony Whyton

OXFORD
UNIVERSITY PRESS

OXFORD
UNIVERSITY PRESS

Oxford University Press is a department of the
University of Oxford. It furthers the University's objective
of excellence in research, scholarship, and education
by publishing worldwide

Oxford   New York
Auckland   Cape Town   Dar es Salaam   Hong Kong   Karachi
Kuala Lumpur   Madrid   Melbourne   Mexico City   Nairobi
New Delhi   Shanghai   Taipei   Toronto

With offices in
Argentina   Austria   Brazil   Chile   Czech Republic   France   Greece
Guatemala   Hungary   Italy   Japan   Poland   Portugal   Singapore
South Korea   Switzerland   Thailand   Turkey   Ukraine   Vietnam

Oxford is a registered trade mark of Oxford University Press
in the UK and certain other countries.

Published in the United States of America by
Oxford University Press
198 Madison Avenue, New York, New York 10016

© Oxford University Press 2013

Library of Congress Cataloging-in-Publication Data
Whyton, Tony.
Beyond A love supreme : John Coltrane and the legacy of an album / Tony Whyton.
    p.   cm
Includes bibliographical references and index.
ISBN 978-0-19-973323-1 (alk. paper) — ISBN 978-0-19-973324-8 (alk. paper)
1. Coltrane, John, 1926–1967. Love supreme.   2. Coltrane, John, 1926–1967—Criticism
and interpretation.   3. Jazz—History and criticism.   I. Title.
ML419.C645W59   2013
788.7'165092—dc23   2012042053

1 3 5 7 9 8 6 4 2

Printed in the United States of America
on acid-free paper

For Fiona, George and Owen

In a sense he is the archetypal 60s artist, the man who reshaped the iconography of jazz genius from the brilliant burnout of Charlie Parker—a 50s beat idea—to that of the abstaining saint, paradoxically meditative and angry, Eastern and yet American. He became the paradigm for the searching artist.[1]

Trane was…music beyond what we conceive music to be.[2]

Readers who believe that records make themselves and that horn players are fed by ravens sent down from heaven, like the prophet Elijah, are advised to pick themselves a less earthbound music to admire. Jazz musicians are professionals. The prejudice against "commercialism" among a large section of the jazz public makes it necessary to repeat this obvious truth.[3]

John was a Buddha and we were his disciples.[4]

I had polio as a young person; that certainly was influential in personal ways but from the standpoint of a human being, developing as a man and as a human being, I really give it to Coltrane, because what that made me see was that there is more than meets the eye, beyond the surface, beyond what you see.[5]

CONTENTS

LIST OF ILLUSTRATIONS

ACKNOWLEDGMENTS

Considering the profound impact of Coltrane's work on musicians, writers, and audiences alike, choosing to write a book about *A Love Supreme* was not an easy decision to make, and I had an early conversation with Coltrane authority Lewis Porter about the idea. In many ways, Lewis's comprehensive study of the life and work of Coltrane makes any subsequent writing appear insignificant, and yet his encouragement and support from the outset was crucial to the development of this study—thank you, Lewis! I would also like to thank my colleagues at the University of Salford for providing me with a stimulating environment for interdisciplinary thinking. George McKay and members of the Salford Jazz Research Group need a special mention, as our regular gatherings and discussions helped to shape some of the themes and approaches within this study. The late David Sanjek was also a keen supporter of this project, providing me with a number of interesting sources and cross-disciplinary takes on Coltrane and the political hotbed of the 1960s. I am particularly grateful to Nicholas Gebhardt, whose enthusiasm for this project, creative ideas, and perspectives on American culture proved invaluable to me at every stage of the writing process.

Over the last few years, I've been fortunate enough to have had informal conversations with distinguished writers and researchers who continue to write groundbreaking scholarship on jazz, including Paul Berliner, Lee Brown, Chuck Hersch, Michael Jarrett, Tom Perchard, Brian Priestley, Alyn Shipton, Alan Stanbridge, Catherine Tackley, and Walter van de Leur, to name but a few—each of these conversations helped to refine some of the ideas within this text. Since 2010, I've also been fortunate to have been working with a distinguished group of European scholars as part of the *Rhythm Changes: Jazz Cultures and European Identities* project, which looks at the role of jazz within different European settings. The research team continually remind me of the need to treat music as a cross-disciplinary practice, and this ethos has certainly fed into the working methods for this study.

Some of the ideas for individual chapters were enhanced as a result of invitations to conferences and academic events. Therefore, I would like to thank Vincent Cotro for setting up the Coltrane Colloquium at the University of Tours in 2007; in many ways, the Tours event demonstrated the breadth of current Coltrane scholarship and helped reinforce the need for this book. Mine Dogantan-Dack deserves a special mention too, not only as a strong advocate of studies into recorded music but also as a supporter of my work over the past few years. I would also like to thank Bjorn Heile for inviting me to participate in the Watching Jazz Conference in Glasgow, and Louise Gibbs, who invited me to present a keynote at the Leeds International Jazz Conference, both in 2011. These conferences provided me with the opportunity to test ideas with different audiences and refine several of the themes that run throughout this study.

The late John Tchicai was incredibly generous with his time, as was Yashuiro Fujioka. I am indebted to friends and colleagues who provided resources, experiences, informal feedback, and snippets of information along the way. In particular, Jeremy Barham, Andrew Beck, Ben Bierman, Andrew Dubber, Krin Gabbard, Jonathan Goh, Russ Hepworth Sawyer, Nick Jones, Wolfram Knauer, Paul McIntyre, Dale Perkins, Tim Wall, and Robert Wilsmore. I would like to thank Suzanne Ryan for being so enthusiastic about this project from the start, and Adam Cohen, Erica Woods Tucker, and the team at Oxford University Press for their patience and professionalism. I would particularly like to thank the anonymous peer reviewers who offered valuable and constructive feedback at every stage of the publication process. Finally, I'd like to thank my family for their continued support and encouragement—in particular, Fiona, who maintains a perfect balance between fantastic wife and critical ally.

Beyond *A Love Supreme*

Beyond *A Love Supreme*

Jazz recordings are powerful objects. The legacy of recorded jazz functions as the backbone of the music's history and shvapes our understanding of the past. Historically, recordings were crucial to the spread of jazz culture, enabling the music to develop into a global phenomenon. Within the early decades of jazz history, entering the recording studio not only provided musicians with an opportunity to document their music for posterity but also encouraged new ways of working and perceiving performance practice. This balance between viewing recordings as a form of historical documentation (capturing music as it would have sounded) and understanding recording as a creative medium (developing sounds that are unique to the studio) points to potential frictions that emerge when jazz is placed on record. Jed Rasula, for example, describes jazz records as a "seductive menace"; they are oxymoronic in that they are, on the one hand, essential to our understanding of the past and, on the other hand, problematic, in that they offer a limited take on the historical process.[1]

As seductive objects, recordings provide us with a window into the time of their creation and, by listening to studio chatter and outtakes and so on, we can understand how recordings were put together and listen in on the creative process as it happened. As a "menace," recordings can present a skewed view of performance as it would have happened within its historical context; for example, we might believe that all performances of early jazz were similarly short or, through the clever use of editing techniques, we might believe in superhuman feats or that musicians can be in two places at once. Consequently, recordings also engender different forms of behavior in people. By reifying jazz—or seeming to turn the music into an object—jazz recordings crystallize standards and turn fleeting moments into benchmark statements for subsequent generations to absorb, imitate, and measure themselves against. As Martin Williams stated,

> Phonograph records are in a sense a contradiction of the meaning of the music. That is, they tend to make permanent and absolute music that is created for the moment, to express the meaning of the moment. On the other hand, records attest that what is made up for the moment *can* survive that moment aesthetically.[2]

Williams touches on some of the inherent contradictions of using recordings as the central pillars of the music's history, for jazz is often heralded as the quintessential improvised music whose essence cannot be captured or documented other than "in the moment." Indeed, within testimonies of jazz history, the recording is often discussed as a poor substitute for the experience of live music, and there is little acknowledgment of the way musicians and historians both rely on recordings to tell the story of jazz and the profound impact recordings can have on musicians and listeners alike.

During the second half of the 20th century, format changes, the growth in discographies, archival resources, collections, and reissues has demonstrated the importance of recordings to jazz history, which has fed into the construction and understanding of jazz as a canonical art form. In many respects, the canonization of jazz would not be possible without a body of recordings to celebrate and revere. Indeed, it is through the notion of the jazz "work" that musical geniuses are most often celebrated and their recordings discussed as timeless masterpieces. In contrast to the growth in canonical readings of jazz history, recordings also provide us with a means of escaping fixed perceptions of artistic culture or historical notions of genius as records are bound up with the collaborative practices of the modern age. In many respects, jazz records and studio practices align themselves with the dawn of the media age, where electronic objects form a central part of our understanding of artistic experience. As Michael Jarrett states,

> Jazz didn't emerge in an oral culture (America is not mythic Africa; jazzmen are not griots). And except as a reaction, jazz is not a response to print technology, since African Americans were routinely denied access to the benefits of published music. Jazz is, in fact, a response to and an effect of electronic culture (radio and records). As surely as cinema, it invented strategies for navigating electronic space. Louis Armstrong isn't a late arriving epic poet; he's an early arriving cyberwriter. He has lessons to teach us about what is to come.[3]

Jarrett seeks to dispel several myths about jazz's links to the past, its orality and place in nature, and instead asserts the music's link to the modern age. The importance of recording technology to the development of the music makes jazz an ideal cultural form from which to understand the role of art today, where most experiences are mediated by technology in some way.

Considering these points, I argue that we need to think of jazz recordings as more than just sonic documents that capture music in the making. They are powerful cultural artifacts that can affect people's lives, inspire future generations, and act as a beacon for social change. More broadly, recordings have political potential both in the way they provide the building blocks for understanding jazz history but also by the way in which their influence extends way beyond musical or even artistic communities.[4] Recordings can be understood both as fixed works that are open to interpretation *and* as performative texts that can be played in any given context, giving rise to new meanings and uses for music. The multifaceted nature of recordings presents a number of challenges for musicologists who, traditionally, have sought to explain the meaning of works as something fixed and have used the deciphering of a musical score as their primary means of analysis. When we understand the variety of uses of recordings and the meanings they generate over time, new modes of analysis are clearly required. In his study of African American music, for example, Guthrie Ramsey discusses the way in which music presents a particular challenge for musicologists today:

> I believe that it becomes a matter of conscience and principle to acknowledge the limits, and indeed try to expand the boundaries, of what is considered the musicological tradition, especially with respect to the study of African American musical culture. We need to couple the sophisticated analytical tools developed in musicology with others in order to reveal the layers of meaning that listeners respond to and find compelling.[5]

Although Ramsey is talking specifically about African American music, I would suggest that a sophisticated toolkit is necessary for all musical study, especially when it involves recordings. I argue that, in order to develop an understanding of the multilayered nature of jazz recordings, a more nuanced form of musicological enquiry needs to be developed where layers of meaning are uncovered and music's place in history is revised and reinterpreted. This study, therefore, reflects a desire to examine the broader contexts within which music operates, the stories that become associated with particular albums or the meanings that have accrued, changed, and transformed over time. By understanding jazz in this way, it is possible to examine how recordings feed into the historicizing process and, in turn, how they both engender a sense of belonging and fuel cultural mythologies.

BEYOND *A LOVE SUPREME*

John Coltrane's *A Love Supreme* provides the perfect model to explore these issues in detail, hence my reason for choosing this album as the subject for this study. Coltrane's suite is, arguably, the most canonical of jazz works; the original recording provides listeners with a definitive masterwork that was produced in a studio environment. The limited nature of alternate versions, including the one live performance of the work, affords the album a unique place among other seminal jazz recordings. Equally, the deeply personal and spiritual content of the album has inspired subsequent generations of musicians and listeners, highlighting the recording's ability to become more than just a reproduction of musical performance. Indeed, *A Love Supreme* has come to fulfill a mythic role in jazz history, being celebrated as the most spiritual of jazz works and creating the illusion of boundaries between Coltrane's music before and after the release of this seminal recording. I developed this study as a means of moving beyond a mere description of the album's content and production and sought to delve into what *A Love Supreme* stands for, how the recording has been perceived over time, and how it makes us think about both jazz history and, more generically, about recordings. Therefore, in moving *Beyond A Love Supreme*, I explore how recordings exert influence on and feed into different types of cultural activity.

In this study, I argue that recordings such as *A Love Supreme* have the potential to problematize conventional understandings of music. As symbols, recordings can come to stand for a whole host of cultural values and mythologies. In many ways, the mythic stories that permeate jazz history lie at the heart of the narrative of *A Love Supreme*. And yet, when viewed discursively, they can be used to challenge existing jazz historiography, uncover underlying ideological viewpoints, and reappraise traditional musicological boundaries.

Therefore, *Beyond A Love Supreme* does not dwell on the examination of the musical "text" or spend a lot of time documenting historical accounts of the album's creation. Over recent years, several studies have been published that provide excellent examples of these approaches, so

I have deliberately avoided duplicating perspectives found in the range of Coltrane publications that are currently available. For example, Lewis Porter's comprehensive biography of John Coltrane includes a substantial analysis of *A Love Supreme*, including a close reading of the suite's formal and thematic characteristics.[6] Equally, Ashley Kahn's book *A Love Supreme: The Creation of John Coltrane's Classic Album* is an insightful and approachable study of the *A Love Supreme* album and offers several interviews, images, and key information on the conception, production, and dissemination of Coltrane's seminal work.[7] Both Porter's and Kahn's texts provide a suitable backdrop to this study and I have drawn on aspects of these works in my attempt to move beyond *A Love Supreme*.

Over recent years, "Coltrane studies" has certainly developed as a distinctive field within jazz scholarship, with a continual stream of publications that seek to reinterpret, revise, and clarify understandings of the artist. These include books, articles, and edited collections that focus on different aspects of Coltrane's life and recordings, from close musical analyses to psychological readings of the artist's biography, from situating the icon within racial discourses to exploring his biography through creative nonfiction.[8] As a body of work, these writings demonstrate the complexity of Coltrane studies today and the breadth of disciplinary perspectives on offer.

In contrast, my focus in this study is to use a multitude of strategies to demonstrate that when we listen to music on record, we are getting much more than a purely sonic experience; the reach of Coltrane moves significantly beyond the boundaries of traditional musicological scholarship. Musician Dave Liebman describes the power and appeal of Coltrane's music, as well as the benefits of revisiting Coltrane's music and finding something new:

> The recordings are a well that will never run dry, much like in music Bach is, Beethoven, Mozart. See, first, it becomes you looking at it from afar, then you get a little closer to it, the light gets a little brighter, you get a little clearer. You start to understand a little bit about it. The light gets really bright then. And then you have to turn around and leave it. But then if you live a long life, you are inevitably drawn back to the light. You have to see it again. You will see it differently of course. And now you see it not so bright, you see it in another kind of way. It is like there is a kind of different color about it. It is like the Tibet in 49 days, you know. The light changes. You go through that border and when you see Coltrane at that point, you realize that this is something beyond words, beyond the music and that keeps you going for what you want to do. That is the

whole point, not the whole tone scale. That is the secondary point. Now that is the deal.[9]

Beyond A Love Supreme takes up this challenge to move beyond existing textual and musical observations. This book is not about music that is recorded for posterity's sake but about the influence of recordings on culture at large; what we hear is only one part of the story. Recordings such as *A Love Supreme* gain a life and momentum of their own that is supported by mythmaking and the mediating forces of history. Therefore, *Beyond A Love Supreme* complements and enhances existing scholarship on Coltrane at the same time as it encourages listeners to think again about what they read or listen to and, indeed, about their own relationship to Coltrane and his music. This book encourages critical listening and an awareness of the cultural impact of the recording both at the time of its creation and beyond the artist's lifetime.

In moving *Beyond A Love Supreme*, I have structured this book as four free-standing chapters that can be read continuously or as individual case studies. In chapter 1, I discuss the common interpretations of Coltrane's suite and the ways in which the album is described in musical terms. I highlight how the album feeds into the established binaries of jazz history, from the balance between the composed and the improvised to the live and the mediated. I conclude by suggesting that *A Love Supreme* provides us with a means of challenging straightforward readings of music and established models of understanding.

In chapter 2, I examine the symbolic importance of *A Love Supreme* within the canon of seminal jazz recordings. Through a detailed analysis of Coltrane literature, musicians' reactions, and the marketing strategies of the Impulse label, I discuss the reification of jazz and the ritualistic value instilled in *A Love Supreme*, and comment on the album's status as an iconic cultural artifact. I illustrate how recordings such as *A Love Supreme* feed into consumer desires for collection, nostalgia, and the deification of artists, and support the ideals of a linear and teleological history. I conclude with a discussion of Coltrane as a deified artist whose masterpiece is situated at the heart of hagiographic depictions of jazz history. Coltrane is often viewed as the conduit for divine inspiration, separated from the everyday world, as opposed to a musician working within specific social conditions and an ever-changing political discourse.

Chapter 3 explores the reception of Coltrane's late works in relation to *A Love Supreme* focusing in particular on *Ascension, Interstellar Space*, and *The Olatunji Concert: The Last Live Recording*. I discuss the way in which the late recordings challenge established musicological methods and problematize dominant representations of Coltrane today. I explore the possible motivations behind the critical reception of the late works and conclude with a discussion of the social and political context in which the albums were created. Finally, I suggest methods of critical listening that both help to situate the recordings in their historical context and which liberate the recordings from the confines of the neo-traditionalist agenda.

The final chapter explores the cultural impact of *A Love Supreme* from the 1970s to the present day. This focuses not only on discussions of musical tributes and reworkings of the seminal album, but also on a study of the album's impact on literature, poetry, and popular culture. I explore ways in which the album has accrued a series of cultural meanings that go beyond the production of Coltrane's sound world, in particular examining *A Love Supreme* as a cultural signifier for truth, honesty, and spirituality, and a trope for individuality, personal struggle, and the quest for inner meaning. Through an examination of the artistic impact and influence of *A Love Supreme*, I examine the way in which the themes of authenticity and universality play off against each other in the representation of the work. I conclude with a demonstration of the ways in which the album has been subject to ideological control and provide examples of recent interpretations of the work that help to shed light on the mythmaking process.

In addition to celebrating the joy that musicians, critics, and audiences alike have experienced when listening to Coltrane's music on record, *Beyond A Love Supreme* examines the mythologies, inherent contradictions, and problems associated with studies of recorded jazz and the particular issues that are unique to *A Love Supreme* and the late Coltrane recordings. As much as musicians and listeners attempt to conceptualize music as an idealized and autonomous experience, I argue throughout that there is no such thing as "the music itself." Recordings, like any other mediating artifact, exist as an integral part of cultural discourse. They operate in a particular marketplace, are consumed differently by different people at different times, and come to represent a host of meanings as they are disseminated and experienced through time. More important, when entering a network of cultural influence and exchange, recordings have the power to change the way in which we think about the world. In *A Love Supreme*'s case, this could mean that the album can change the way in which we perceive the 1960s or how we rethink the relationship between race and spirituality or, indeed, how we view the world before the album came into existence.

Upon completing this manuscript, I came across a report on the BBC about John Coltrane's former house in Dix Hills where the artist created *A Love Supreme*.[10] The feature discussed the desire to transform the house—which has been virtually untouched since the 1960s—into a cultural center for jazz. The report focused on the way in which the presence of *A Love Supreme* could be felt within the upstairs of the house and the way in which an initiative such as a Coltrane cultural center could serve to rejuvenate an interest in live jazz at a time of decreasing audiences. After watching the report, I was struck by the way in which the news item reinforced several of the themes that are explored in this book. For example, several Coltrane mythologies linked to the artist's biography and the creation of *A Love Supreme* were presented without question, and, although 50 years have passed since Coltrane created his seminal album, I was fascinated by the way in which the music was used to make sense of the present, forming the basis of a strategy for rescuing jazz in a period of decline; surprisingly, the report did not enter into a discussion about the balance between past and present, the effects of the canonization of jazz, or the impact the Coltrane legacy has on musicians working today. More than anything, the report showed how Coltrane's music—and *A Love Supreme* in particular—continues to have currency today and provides people with a way of understanding the past as well as envisaging the future of jazz.

Moving beyond *A Love Supreme*, therefore, presents a challenge for us to think about ways in which recordings not only provide musicians and audiences with profound listening experiences but also how music carries a symbolic value that can help to explain societal relationships, the construction and spread of culture, and our understandings of the past, present, and future. When we understand the cultural dynamics of recordings, the way in which they reflect and trigger social movements, influence different artistic pursuits, or are used in the musicking of people, we begin to appreciate the power of jazz on record and the potential of music to affect change.

CHAPTER 1

ELATION—ELEGANCE—EXALTATION

Jazz history is often constructed around antonymic concepts and categories. Dichotomies are used to establish the authenticity of jazz and to promote an idealized view of the music's past. The presence of antonyms—or binaries—within jazz discourse can be understood as essential to the mythmaking process, playing a central role in promoting great jazz of the past as simple and noncontradictory, natural artworks that are devoid of conflict and contestation. More than any other narrative device, the antonym affirms a sense of boundary within jazz, serving to explain what is celebrated, revered, and documented as important historically. In effect, binaries create a boundary between what is considered jazz and what is excluded. As Krin Gabbard suggests, an agreed set of dualisms are an essential part of creating the canonical discourse we are presented with today:

> Although they violently disagreed on the definition of jazz, critics in the 1940s tacitly agreed to fight their battles around a set of dualisms—black versus white, art versus commerce, nature versus culture, technique versus affect, European versus native—on which claims about jazz as art have been built ever since.[1]

Whereas Gabbard stresses the way in which binaries shape the jazz narrative and cement perceptions of authentic practice, these dualisms can largely be understood as a cultural construct. For example, in his book *Jazz in American Culture*, Peter Townsend argues that jazz history is littered with examples of a lack of fit between jazz practices and the established cultural categories found within jazz writings. As an example, Townsend states:

The division between "improvisation" and "composition" illustrates some of the problems that emerge.... Jazz is the prime, even the stereotypical, example of an improvisation-based music. When composition appears in jazz, it is therefore problematic because of its designation into the opposite category.[2]

For Townsend, jazz's supposed authenticity can be measured through a series of micro-myths, established propositions that inevitably fall into oppositional categories (such as creativity is a male and not a female domain, or jazz is improvised and not composed).[3] Therefore, I argue that the essence of jazz—or the music's authenticity—is predominantly asserted by stressing the music's links to African American history and a separation from the influence of white European culture.

While the African American influence is central to understanding the development of jazz historically, the continuation of African American exceptionalist readings of the music today often leads to jazz being represented in essentialist terms. Using binary categories to establish a form of idealized purity typifies the way in which mythologies become naturalized or subliminally woven into the fabric of jazz culture. For example, consider Leonard L. Brown's statement on the music of John Coltrane, published in 2010:

The process of transmission of musical knowledge and practices within black American culture in both rural and urban situations had its own belief system that guided and set rules for music making.... Once he became a member of this inner circle, Coltrane learned the old time ways, the current ways and probably even glimpses into the future.[4]

Brown lays claim to Coltrane's life and music from an insider perspective, promoting the notion of an essential black subject and the belief that black culture is uniform, and experienced collectively. Brown borrows from writers such as Portia Maultsby to demonstrate "the biases of primarily white writers, whose cultural orientation limited their capacities to critically assess the social significance of the Black music tradition."[5] Within this context, the question of what constitutes a "cultural orientation" is both problematic and reductive. This perspective assumes that racial identity foregrounds every other type of social identity category from gender to class to geography to educational training, and serves to exclude people from accessing an "authentic" culture. The reductive nature of this discourse not only denies alternative voices to comment on and inform black cultural experience, it also limits the representation of iconic figures such as John Coltrane. These perspectives create the skewed feeling of an authentic voice, appropriating the Coltrane legacy in order to perpetuate a view of jazz as an exclusive, spiritual, African American music, where only a select few can gain access to the riches of the music and its culture. As "You Have to Be Invited," the title to Brown's introduction to his Coltrane volume, makes clear, ownership and understanding of Coltrane, and broader black American culture, is mutually exclusive, literally a black-and-white affair. Arguably, by simplifying Coltrane's contribution to jazz history to the level of a spiritual black signifier, these readings do not enable scholars to engage with Coltrane in ways that are polysemic.

Coltrane's life and music *are* complex, sophisticated, and at times contradictory, which, I argue, means they are resistant to simple oppositions. I would also suggest that the heterogeneous nature of the Coltrane legacy has enabled his music to resonate with different groups, retaining significant cultural currency up until the present day. Black culture is not monolithic, and, within today's cosmopolitan world, the boundaries of race are continually blurred and problematized. Ironically, Coltrane's legacy, rather than reinforcing the notion of the essential black subject, provides us with a model for dismantling reified notions of blackness, as I discuss later on.

In addition to the portrayal of jazz as an essential black music, dominant antonyms would include the following assumptions about jazz practice: jazz is art music and not commercially oriented popular music, the music is improvised not composed, recorded jazz is a pale imitation of live jazz, creativity in jazz is a masculine enterprise not feminine, jazz is acoustic not electronic, it is soulful and corporeal not cerebral, American not European, and so on. The canonization of jazz has served to cement these categories and present jazz history and the concept of "The Tradition" as unchanging and uncontested. Binaries help to convey a false sense of truth and objectivity and enable music history to be constructed around the values of a dominant social group or power structure. Since the 1990s, and Scott Deveaux's celebrated essay "Constructing the Jazz Tradition," several jazz scholars have attempted to challenge the established interpretation of jazz history with alternative readings or oppositional approaches to jazz scholarship. For example, although radically different in terms of underlying methodology, agenda and style, writers including David Ake, E. Taylor Atkins, Richard Sudhalter, and Sherrie Tucker have sought to offer alternative readings of jazz history and to dispel the myths surrounding jazz practice and established binaries.[6] However, within the dominant discourse, the antonymic categorization of jazz is still the primary means of establishing the essence of the music. Moreover, several writers working within critical contexts of the New Jazz Studies, although themselves often examining the constructed nature of jazz narratives, continue to fall back on established dichotomies and antonymic concepts.[7]

A LOVE SUPREME

John Coltrane's *A Love Supreme*, recorded in 1964, is a fascinating album with which to explore the way in which binaries help to shape our understanding of jazz and fuel the mythmaking process. *A Love Supreme* is continually discussed in antonymic terms, and yet, perhaps more than any other recording, the album challenges many of the binaries that form the basis of dominant jazz narratives. Indeed, through an examination of the album and its place within jazz history, I demonstrate how *A Love Supreme* is problematic when viewing jazz history through established binaries. The album foregrounds the recorded status of jazz, inverting the primacy of the live performance and encourages us to consider the album as a jazz creation in its own right, as opposed to a document that provides a snapshot of jazz performance as it would have sounded in a live setting. Indeed, the only complete live version of *A Love Supreme*, recorded by the Classic Quartet at the 1965 Antibes Juan les Pins Festival, offers a different conception of the music and is more akin to other extended live performances of the time. The studio recording is calculated and engineered, designed to convey and construct a specific message, within the relative rigidity of the studio environment. As Lewis Porter states, "The studio recording, as issued, remains the definitive statement of the musical and spiritual aspirations of this quiet, unassuming man."[8] Musically, *A Love Supreme* is frequently discussed in binary terms. Take, for example, Porter's reading of the form and structure of the album (see figure 1.1). Porter describes *A Love Supreme* as having a certain symmetry or binary structure, the four movements being divided into two distinct halves (a 2+2 structure) with the harmonic and thematic material feeding directly into this model.

As part of his analysis, Porter describes the way in which the *A Love Supreme* theme is featured primarily in part I of the suite ("Acknowledgement") and then again, albeit slightly amended, in part III of the suite ("Pursuance"). Porter uses the structural diagram to suggest that there is harmonic symmetry at play within tonal centers of each movement and that the underlying plan provides the suite with a clear sense of unity. Porter identifies a series of tonal relationships that

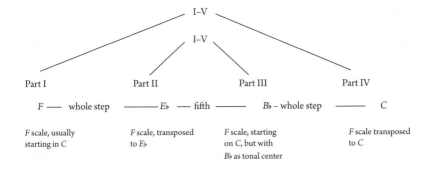

Figure 1.1:
Lewis Porter's tonal plan for *A Love Supreme*.

work between movements as well as shaping the overall design of the suite, from the movement of a whole step to fifth to whole step between movements to the overarching tonic to dominant relationships that link part I to part IV, and part II to part III. Although this works as one reading of the suite, tonal and thematic relationships are present throughout the album and the notion of symmetry works only in certain ways. Indeed, formal symmetry could be said to work only at the harmonic level as thematic relationships between parts correspond in different ways: part I has no thematic relationship to part IV, and relates more closely to the material presented in part III.

A more interesting question revolves around why symmetry and unity are desirable concepts with which to frame *A Love Supreme* in the first place. I would argue that seeking out a sense of unity and symmetrical patterns in this way is symptomatic of a particular discourse, most closely aligned to formalist musicology. Further, while these methods provide one reading of the work, I would argue that they can work against alternative readings of the music and, at times, run contrary to its aural impact, and the way in which the music is experienced sonically. When listening to the recording of *A Love Supreme*, alternative readings of the music could legitimately be offered in which features such as form and structure are experienced differently.[9] Moreover, even when transcribing the music and drawing on western notation to describe and analyze the musical material, a certain selectivity leads to the reinforcement of themes of unity and the underlying ideological discourse of *A Love Supreme* as spiritual art music. For example, take the introductory saxophone flourish that opens the *A Love Supreme* suite: this is most often described as a fanfare-like introduction to the suite, setting the scene for the spiritual experience to follow. As Ashley Kahn writes:

Whether blown from minarets or at military barracks, as a call to prayer or to arms, it's a time-honored device with a timeless function. Fanfares demand attention, heralding the importance of the message to follow....In the context of *A Love Supreme*, Coltrane's warmly stated opening figure—in E major, which, though briefly played, was an unusual key for Coltrane—serves as a benediction, a spiritual welcome.[10]

Kahn's statement imbues Coltrane's opening with spiritual significance, aligning the fanfare with politics and religion, and citing the "unusual" key signature as a unique feature of the work.

The unique characteristics of the opening are also discussed by Ravi Coltrane:

In "Acknowledgement," John uses two sets of harmonic relationships or melodic "cells." The opening motif is built on one: it's a 1–2–5 cell (1 being the root of a major scale, 2 the first degree above it, 5 the fifth) in E major, which he begins on the fifth. Later, he revisits this cell in the main melody—ba-dwee-dah, ba-DWEE-dah—as 5–2–1, first in the key of F and then B-flat....If John only used these particular cells in *A Love Supreme*, that would be one thing. These melodic cells may have had much representational value for him because they began to appear in various ways in much of his music after the suite was recorded.[11]

Ravi Coltrane asserts the importance of these cells to Coltrane's output from *A Love Supreme* onward and stresses the symbolic importance of these motifs, suggesting Coltrane had discovered something deeper about music. He continues:

So I thought about those cells as pure numbers and saw how they define ratios known as the Golden Mean, also called the divine proportion. These ratios are found in proportions of the human body and in nature: in seashells, when trees begin branching. It's also an established theory of aesthetic perfection: how buildings or portraits are arranged, or when events occur in Mozart sonatas.[12]

To conclude, Ravi Coltrane suggests that these cells have a deep symbolic meaning that reaches beyond the music itself and demonstrates Coltrane's desire to create a universal language in music and to "call together the most basic and divine qualities that are common to all human experience."[13]

As with any reading of musical content, both Kahn's and Ravi Coltrane's interpretations are governed by an externally imposed ideological agenda that promotes certain aspects of Coltrane's music and philosophy over others. In order to demonstrate this, consider the following transcription of Coltrane's opening fanfare:

Figure 1.2:
A Love Supreme—John Coltrane's opening "fanfare" phrase.

Contrary to Ravi Coltrane's statement that this motif was unique to *A Love Supreme* and shaped the later works of Coltrane, the opening fanfare material is not unusual at all, but closely mirrors the theme to *My Favorite Things* both in terms of underlying single chord and motivic structure:

Figure 1.3:
My Favorite Things, bars 1–9 (5–2–1 cells).

When playing this passage, the thematic and harmonic relationship to *My Favorite Things* is clear. Indeed, the 1–2–5 motivic cell that Ravi Coltrane describes provides the building blocks for *My Favorite Things and A Love Supreme*. Furthermore, the motivic links between the two pieces move beyond the opening fanfare, as the first 9 bars of *My Favorite Things* sound out the same intervals (albeit transposed) as Coltrane's *A Love* Supreme theme (da-bwee-dah):

Figure 1.4:
A Love Supreme opening melody (transposed for comparison) and 5–2–1 cell structure.

We need to consider why these connections are not discussed in any of the Coltrane literature. Both Kahn's and Ravi Coltrane's statements stress the importance of these cell structures, which might well be true.

However, in positing these ideas, they use signifiers that serve to detach *A Love Supreme* from the works that preceded it. In concentrating on the spiritual significance of the motifs, the way the music feeds into concepts of perfection, divine proportions, nature, and even Mozart, Coltrane is automatically elevated in status; these signifiers serve to promote Coltrane as a spiritually inspired artistic genius who is separated from the everyday world of commerce and industry. To compare Coltrane's *My Favorite Things* with *A Love Supreme* at a musical level does not suit the master narrative at play. The *My Favorite Things* motif was performed almost constantly by Coltrane throughout the 1960s, and it would not be far-fetched to suggest that this cell was embedded within Coltrane's musical routine, his muscle memory and formed part of his musical consciousness. However, to suggest an influence of this popular melody on the opening of *A Love Supreme* would seem at odds with the conception of the suite as it challenges several of the established mythologies surrounding the work's creation. At once, the music would be regarded as intertextual and not a singular original, and the suggestion of tying the recording to any aspect of Coltrane's popular hit would jar with the spiritual and political conception of the album.

Equally, other musical traits are not discussed within writings on *A Love Supreme*. The title of Part II, "Resolution," for example, is often discussed in spiritual terms, feeding off the narrative of Coltrane's resolution to follow the path of God. And yet, at a basic musical level, resolution can also be understood as a literal study in musical resolution. The "Resolution" theme is not only made up of a descending phrase that is repeated four times, each with a slightly different ending, but also the melodic contour moves from tonic to the tritone and back again, reinforcing the notion of tension and resolution in musical terms. As a descending figure, the resolution theme is suggestive of its title, moving far away from the tonal center before moving back again.

Formal Plan

Formally, Porter emphasizes the symmetrical qualities of the suite by describing *A Love Supreme* as a 2+2 structure (see figure 1.5). While this reading works perfectly well, I am interested in exploring ways in which the structure of the album—or experiences of structure—can change according to context and format. For example, when considering the album as a purely sonic document, the structure of the material could well be governed by the practicalities of the listening experience.

On vinyl, *A Love Supreme* divides evenly on to two sides, reinforcing Porter's 2+2 feel. However, when listening to the album on CD or other digital formats, the continuous nature of the experience could lead to other interpretations of form and structure.

At a basic level, the lack of track listing for part IV encourages the listener to perceive "Psalm" as something separate and distinct from the earlier three sections. Also, when viewing the album as a type of religious offering, the 3+1 structure works well: the first three parts feed off active nouns, in that they relate to verb forms ("Acknowledgement," "Resolution," "Pursuance"), and are multilayered in meaning and also suggestive of forms of religious observance. By describing Part IV as a psalm, Coltrane separates the final movement from the previous sections and treats the material in a radically different way. In his liner notes to the album, Coltrane also describes "Psalm" in terms that differ from the opening three parts, stating that it is a "musical narration of the theme, 'A LOVE SUPREME.'"[14]

Musically, the structure does not have to be read as symmetrical either, with the first three parts containing regular meters, identifiable chordal vamps, and progressions, and employing rhythm conventionally. Within the first three sections, the rhythm section perform in a fairly traditional way, keeping time and accompanying Coltrane either by reacting to his playing or being proactive, driving the tempo or interjecting phrases or solo sections within the musical dialogue. However, "Psalm" is a different experience altogether. Led purely by Coltrane, the movement is not governed by a particular feel or meter and as such,

Part	Title	Section Characteristics
I	"Acknowledgement"	Opening fanfare figure followed by Latin feel. *A Love Supreme* motif featured over vamp, transposed into 12 keys, and "A Love Supreme" spoken in chant-like manner.
II	"Resolution"	Theme is a descending blues-oriented phrase. Can be understood as a musical exploration of resolution, a repeated phrase with modified ending, movement away from tonal center to the tritone and back.
III	"Pursuance"	Minor blues with fast swing feel. The theme draws on the three-note *A Love Supreme* motivic cell.
IV	"Psalm"	Musical setting of Coltrane's poem *A Love Supreme*. Rhythm section plays a subservient role—pedal tones and single-chord vamp employed with free tempo and meter.

Figure 1.5:
A Love Supreme **movement characteristics.**

produces a feeling of free time. As has been documented elsewhere, the album version of "Psalm" is unique in terms of Coltrane's repertoire in that it provides a musical rendition of his *A Love Supreme* poem, featured in the liner notes to the album. The literal *sounding out* of Coltrane's dedication to God produces a synergy between the artist's words and music that governs the structure and delivery of the material for the final part. We have a movement away from the abstract world of the blues, Afro-Cuban, or swing feel of earlier sections toward an overt literary statement expressed in musical terms. In this respect, the 3+1 structure is just as convincing as a 2+2 format although suggestive of a different listening experience. Whether describing *A Love Supreme* as a 2+2 structure or 3+1 depends largely on the desires of the listener; ultimately, this observation demonstrates that interpretations of form are liable to change depending on the technological format and on how music is both experienced and read socially.

NEUTRALIZING THE BINARY

Binaries and discussions of unity are deeply entwined, as both concepts encourage us to think in straightforward and easily delineated terms: for example, unity can be contrasted with disunity, and tension results in resolution. And yet, when examining *A Love Supreme* as a type of critical discourse, it becomes apparent how easily the boundaries between antonyms can become blurred or how binaries are continually modified, changed, and adapted to feed into broader mythic jazz concepts or underlying narratives. Writings on *A Love Supreme* tend to carefully negotiate established dualisms in order to preserve the integrity of the album and its place within jazz's canonical history. In other words, in order for the story of *A Love Supreme* to retain a degree of unity and unquestionable authenticity, a certain degree of control, promotion, and manipulation of the narrative takes place using established binaries selectively to promote particular interpretations of events. And yet it is important to examine how each antonym, or the boundaries of the discourse, changes according to what type of activity is being described or what mythologies are being reinforced within the Coltrane biography or *A Love Supreme* story. For the following section, I offer several examples of how *A Love Supreme* both fuels and challenges antonymic concepts in jazz, exploring how mythic concepts play out in writings on the album and broader musical discourse.

Composition/Improvisation

A good example of the way in which binaries shift according to context can be seen when *A Love Supreme* is described either as a composition or an improvisation. Conventionally, jazz is foregrounded as a live improvised art that is the product of spontaneous creation and inspired performers. When great jazz compositions are created, they provide a wealth of material for musicians to play on, and are most often celebrated through the "liveness" of particular performances; one only has to think of the way in which great Ellington compositions are often linked to special performances or venues (the Cotton Club, Newport, Westminster Abbey, etc.) to get a feel for how composition is still framed in performative terms. With this in mind, the concept of jazz composition is still problematic when the micro-myth of jazz as "in the moment" is evoked. Liveness, improvisation, and spontaneity are often promoted as key tenets of great jazz performance that serve to separate the music both from the calculated, rational, and, by implication, sterile and contrived world of western classical music, and from the overly produced, predictable and formulaic sounds of popular music.[15] Even when recordings of jazz are produced, the emphasis is still often placed on the magic of the recording venue or the energy of the studio environment.

Myths bound up with seminal recordings such as *Kind of Blue*, for example, promote spontaneity and liveness of performances in order to subvert the edited, engineered, mediated, or produced nature of recordings themselves. Recordings such as these are described as unique, one-off events that capture something magical. Indeed, when describing the way in which great jazz recordings are born, there is a general desire to promote materials as spontaneous. This is usually achieved by stating that musicians often worked with little or no rehearsal time, that compositions were written in the studio or just prior to a recording date, that producers and engineers played a passive role in the recording process and did not interfere with the intentions of the group, that artists performed with compositional sketches only or hardly used any written materials in performance, and that works were recorded in one take. Recordings also promote liveness, the energy or atmosphere of a particular venue or event. This is not only applicable to live recordings (such as Coltrane's *Live at the Village Vanguard*, *Ellington at Newport 1956*, Benny Goodman's *Carnegie Hall Concert 1938*, etc.), but also plays a role in the mythmaking of seminal studio albums. The Rudy van Gelder studio in Englewood Cliffs, for example, has become a shrine to jazz, a mythic recording space that gave birth to recordings such as *A Love Supreme.*

Although improvisation or liveness is still foregrounded in descriptions of seminal recordings, the growing canonical status of jazz means that "works" (or jazz compositions) are fulfilling a more central role in the story of jazz. Seminal recordings not only reify great historical performances, they are today treated in a similar way to classical compositions, with the singular artist being favored above the group and recordings functioning as a type of score that fixes performance styles and encourages imitation and reenactment.[16] The presence of great jazz works demonstrates that the music has transcended its status as a mere product of popular culture and ascended to the heights of art music or, in the case of Coltrane, it is music touched by the divine. The coexistence of different types of narrative challenges traditional versions of authentic jazz practice as being improvised instead of composed; paradoxically, seminal jazz recordings are both grounded in the social—as they are a product of group dynamics, political and social circumstances—and treated as autonomous, in that they are considered transcendent of time and space. With *A Love Supreme*, the extent to which the recording is discussed as composed or improvised is continually negotiated and adapted according to what part of the *A Love Supreme* story is being adhered to.

To give an indication of the way in which the *A Love Supreme* narrative is changed and adapted, first consider Alice Coltrane's widespread account of the album's creation:

> It was like Moses coming down from the mountain, it was so beautiful. He walked down and there was that joy, that peace in his face, tranquillity. So I said, "Tell me everything, we didn't see you really for four or five days... ." He said, "This is the first time that I have received all of the music for what I want to record, in a suite. This is the first time I have everything, everything ready."[17]

Alice Coltrane describes the conception of *A Love Supreme* in biblical terms and describes the way in which John Coltrane composed the work during a period of self-imposed isolation. Coltrane had famously locked himself away for five days in order to receive the work; again, the emphasis on the word "receive" promotes Coltrane as a conduit through which God speaks and *A Love Supreme* as a kind of divine offering. The Moses analogy and surrounding narrative feeds into the creation myth of *A Love Supreme* and marks the work as something special and spiritually symbolic. Coltrane's isolation confirms the autonomous status of the artwork: the music has been created away from the influence of the everyday world; it has transcended the social. Furthermore, the conception of the work moves beyond mere musical creativity as it has been touched by the presence of God. As a product of genius, the birth of *A Love Supreme* mirrors other artistic narratives from the myth of Beethoven as the isolated genius, to Stravinsky describing himself as a vessel through which the *Rite of Spring* flowed. The creation myth associated with *A Love Supreme* is enhanced by the assertion that, for the first time in his career, Coltrane produced a perfectly conceived composition prior to entering the studio. This not only provides *A Love Supreme* with a unique status in relation to other Coltrane outputs, but also confirms Coltrane as the sole composer: this work is not about collaboration or group dynamics; it is a personal account of Coltrane's conversance with, and devotion to, God. After his five days in isolation, Coltrane had completed a score that detailed all aspects of the composition.

The details of this manuscript remained undisclosed until a couple of years ago, as Ben Ratliff states:

> A manuscript showing this preliminary musical arrangement for *A Love Supreme* surfaced in late 2004, when Alice Coltrane ... offered it to Guernsey's Auction House to be sold. It indicated, among other things, that Coltrane felt the piece could be arranged for a group of nine: tenor saxophone and "one other horn," piano, trap drums, two basses, two conga players, and one timbales player. Other markings on the paper demonstrate his thoughts: toward the end of part one, he noted, a saxophone solo with quartet accompaniment should lead into "all drums multiple meters and voices changing motif in E♭mi 'A Love Supreme.' ... At the bottom of the page he writes: "last chord to sound like final chord of Alabama."[18]

Coltrane's composition is well conceived. Indeed, Ratliff suggests that the characteristics identified on the score were realized, even if the final version was only for a quartet. *A Love Supreme* has a creation story that describes the production of the piece and an authenticated manuscript to back it up, cementing the work's status as Coltrane's magnum opus, probably his most prolific composition. Even without the biblical analogy, the classical proportions of *A Love Supreme* lead to a position where the work is treated as more "composed" than other Coltrane projects, and the production of the work ties into Coltrane's own desire to write larger-scale forms that move away from jazz standards.[19]

Paul Berliner, for example, describes the chant-like and repetitious quality of "Acknowledgement" as being at odds with most jazz compositions to date and aligns the piece more with classical compositional practice. Berliner draws on the following quote from Barry Kernfeld to illustrate his point:

> Jazz musicians define motivic development according to their own conventions, typically avoiding "the kind of systematic repetition and transposition heard in classical music." Exceptions to this are in such works as Coltrane's suite "A Love Supreme," whose first movement is built upon the constant repetition of a motive, "eventually transposing it into all 12 keys."[20]

As a composed piece, *A Love Supreme* functions to confirm Coltrane's status as a divinely inspired genius whose work has stood the test of time.

And yet, when the *A Love Supreme* narrative moves into detailing the recording session, a second creation myth takes hold and the music is celebrated for a completely different set of qualities. Consider the following passages describing statements from members of the Classic Quartet, featured in Ashley Kahn's book on *A Love Supreme:*

> John said very little about what he wanted. If he had certain specifics that he wanted to add to the music or how he wanted it played, he would say it. I think this is so important, because it was an on-the-spot improvisation, honestly approached music, with nothing pretentious about it at all.[21]
>
> That first day, he didn't have any extra people around.... We didn't have any written music, he'd have some notes that he'd refer to, but as far as the rest of us were concerned, we'd just follow what he did.[22]

These statements provide a stark contrast to Alice Coltrane's account, which claimed that Coltrane had composed *A Love Supreme* in its entirety prior to entering the studio. Paradoxically, we move from one narrative in which the suite has been received and all parts are written, to a different narrative in which, following Coltrane's lead, the Classic Quartet was confronted with limited amounts of material. Even when photographic evidence shows composed notes being used as part of the session, they are played down or dismissed as inconsequential.

Ashley Kahn, for example, underscores a photograph of Jimmy Garrison and Coltrane looking at some notated music with the caption "Coltrane, Garrison, and perhaps some very sparse musical instructions."[23] Obviously, as was probably the case, Coltrane could have conceived the piece in its entirety and conveyed his compositional ideas orally and, as such, the pre- and postrecording testimonies do not necessarily have to be mutually exclusive. However, the overriding narrative coming through from accounts of the *A Love Supreme* recording session is one of spontaneity and improvisation.

Tyner's words in the foregoing quotation, for example, state that improvisation and honesty go hand in hand and, by implication, that precomposed music is somehow contrived or dishonest. There is a deep-felt desire to portray the recording as a unique event that could not be recaptured, and one that had little interference from those outside the quartet. With this in mind, the need to promote the album as being recorded in one take becomes a dominant theme designed to capture the liveness of the work. Elvin Jones's statement that on the first day they didn't have any additional people around refers to the participation of Archie Shepp and Art Davis, who joined the quartet on the second recording date but whose material did not feature on the original release. Jones lays claim to a special atmosphere where the quartet remained undisturbed and able to create music without any additional interference. Even engineer Rudy van Gelder displays a desire to evoke the spontaneity and one-take idea theme when remembering the session: "I don't remember him doing a lot of takes....It's possible I've forgotten some details but I don't remember that. Actually, what I did like about working for him [Coltrane] is he knew when he had it right."[24] Ironically, despite the *A Love Supreme* sessions being recorded over two days and including several outtakes and alternate takes, different personnel, and the subsequent insertion of overdubbed fragments, the "one-take" theme is still prevalent in the story of the album's conception.

A clear example of the way in which the *A Love Supreme* narrative is changed and adapted can be seen in Alice Coltrane's interview with Branford Marsalis, recorded as part of the supporting material for Marsalis's *A Love Supreme Live in Amsterdam* DVD published in 2003. During the interview, Alice Coltrane is asked to recount the story of the conception of *A Love Supreme* and repeats the widespread account of the album's creation again, using the same Moses analogy and view of *A Love Supreme* as composed work and anecdotal structure as cited in Kahn earlier. Although Alice Coltrane must have repeated this story on endless occasions—it is featured in most biographies and writings on the creation of the album—to the point where it is fairly fixed as an anecdote in both form and content, the following dialogue occurs straight after the familiar anecdote and, subsequently, brings the two authenticating creation myths into conflict:

ALICE COLTRANE: About, I would imagine, maybe a few days to a week, he came downstairs like Moses coming down from the mountain and he said, "For the first time in my life, for the next album," he said, "I have *all* of the music… and this is the first time it's ever happened to me." And I thought that was so great because John as himself—how many times he would arrive at the session and he didn't have any music. No music, no song titles, nothing—but would compose the whole album in the hallway.

BRANFORD MARSALIS: I'm a fan of that kind of thing myself, actually. Well, my songs weren't as good as his but I am definitely a fan of showing up and creating songs for the moment.

ALICE COLTRANE: And sometimes they're the best. Sometimes they are because they're fresh, you know, energy, consciousness levels are up high. But you know how it is when we record. After about the second take, you don't wanna hear it any more.[25]

In her retelling of the story, Alice Coltrane states that Coltrane had everything prepared, in contrast to typical recording sessions that would be devised and delivered in the studio, and suggests that there was a certain relief in not having to go into the studio underprepared. Following this statement, we have the interjection from Branford Marsalis, who states that he prefers working by the seat of his pants in order to keep recordings fresh and spontaneous. Suddenly, this response presents us with a clash of two narrative strategies and moves the conversation away from the context of the composed to reasserting the spontaneity of performance, the limited takes and liveness that are established markers of jazz as a form of unmediated expression. Surprisingly, Alice Coltrane switches away from the well-trodden anecdote to concur with Marsalis, leaving the viewer wondering what this change of position means when interpreting A Love Supreme. Does the fact that it was precomposed devalue the music in this context?

The tension between A Love Supreme as fully composed suite and A Love Supreme as spontaneous creation demonstrates the way in which jazz discourse changes and adapts according to the particular values and myths that are being promoted at any given time. When micro-myths come into conflict, the jazz narrative is adapted and certain themes come to the fore while others blend into the background; this means that A Love Supreme can exist as both composed suite and improvised act without the need for resolution. The conflict is touched on by Lewis Porter in his influential essay "A Love Supreme: Jazz Composition as Improvisation." However, Porter's argument does not deal with the tension between these binary categories. Indeed, his essay is designed to appeal to different readerships. On the one hand, *A Love Supreme* is promoted as a composition to rival classical music and give weight to jazz as a legitimate musicological subject. On the other hand, Coltrane's mastery as an improviser is celebrated in order to mark him as unique in the jazz world. In addition to Porter's interpretation of Coltrane's composition as improvisation, I would argue that the examples offered so far demonstrate how *A Love Supreme* can provide a way into challenging existing binary conceptions of jazz. Indeed, the album can serve to deconstruct the composition-improvisation antonym altogether and offer new ways into conceiving musical practice.

In his book *Drifting on a Read: Jazz as a Model for Writing*, Michael Jarrett examines and analyses what he describes as "jazzography"—the associated body of writings and understandings of the music—in order to challenge existing representations of jazz. In moving beyond the confines of musicology, Jarrett explores a range of cultural, contextual, and discursive influences within jazz texts that feed into several master tropes, narrative themes that dominate our understanding of the music. Like Gabbard's and Townsend's earlier discussions of antonyms, Jarrett reiterates the way in which jazz discourse is shaped by binaries and draws on literary theory to challenge the supposedly naturalized dualisms that exist in writings on jazz. Jarrett talks specifically about a handful of tropes that serve to support "jazzology" and romantic understandings of the music. He seeks to dissolve the binary between composition and improvisation, using what he describes as the "obbligato trope" to question what counts as improvisation, composition, and incidental music and to ask, what things take shape in the name of improvisation? His suggestion is that what is described as improvisation, composition, or incidental music is born out of convention and the value systems at play within a given genre. These questions, because they signal a shift in focus from ontology to politics and discourse, result in Jarrett arguing that "any and all distinctions between composition and improvisation are socially constructed and ultimately incomplete."[26]

Jarrett's work is reminiscent of the work of Jacques Derrida, who suggested that, essentially, binaries work as part of ideology or power structure. Derrida's position is here summarized by John Storey: "[Binaries] are not pure opposites—each is *motivated* by the other, ultimately dependent on the absent other for its own presence and meaning.... Simply to reverse the binary opposition would be to keep in place the assumptions already constructed by the opposition."[27]

Derrida argued that we must move beyond the mere reversal of binary oppositions as "one of the two terms controls the other...holds the superior position. To deconstruct the opposition [we must]...overthrow the hierarchy."[28]

When applying Jarrett's ideas to *A Love Supreme*, we can understand the terms composition and improvisation as discursive; they are employed at particular times to perpetuate certain jazz myths. The dominance of improvisation over composition might remain a popular way of understanding jazz practice. However, the canonical presence of albums such as *A Love Supreme* means that the composed elements of the suite are presented as of equal importance. Unlike Porter, who attempted to describe improvisation as a type of composition, Jarrett's approach leads us to a position where we must call into question the very use of the terms "composition" and "improvisation" in the first place, suggesting that they fulfill a particular semantic and political role in jazz. Terminology is not innocent: signs connote as much as they denote, and therefore the use of these terms suggests particular values that underpin the music. Through an analysis of Coltrane narratives and creation myths associated with *A Love Supreme*, it becomes possible to recognize this and to neutralize the binary and, by so doing, to argue for a different way of understanding music.

Drugs/Spiritual Enlightenment

During the year 1957, I experienced, by the grace of God, a spiritual awakening which was to lead me to a richer, fuller, more productive life.[29]

Another binary that fuels the *A Love Supreme* story is the contrast between Coltrane's drug use and his spiritual awakening. Indeed, the *A Love Supreme* narrative draws both on explicit and implicit references to the drugs–divine binary. The album itself is presented as a divine offering and is widely recognized as Coltrane's most personal work, born out of the artist's faith in God and the celebration of his triumph over adversity. In his liner notes to the album, Coltrane describes his epiphany where, in order to overcome his alcohol and heroin addiction, he reconnected with God and found the path to a spiritual life: *A Love Supreme* is presented as a celebration of this significant event and an affirmation of faith.

More implicitly, there is a clear narrative symmetry between the events of 1957 and the creation of *A Love Supreme* in 1964. Coltrane spent five days in self-imposed isolation in order to withdraw from drugs, going cold turkey. It was during this period that Coltrane made his connection with God and asked "to be given the means and privilege to make others happy through music."[30] He emerged from this period a changed person with a renewed sense of purpose and determination, and *A Love Supreme* is an offering designed to acknowledge this life-altering moment. Furthermore, the process of composing *A Love Supreme* echoes the previous period of cold turkey isolation, with Coltrane withdrawing to his room for five days in order to "receive" the work. A narrative symmetry is conveyed where Coltrane embarks on a solitary period of self-discovery and conversance with God; the first period of isolation results in Coltrane's renewal or spiritual rebirth and the second period results in the creation of *A Love Supreme*. Both stories tie together in taking Coltrane away from the everyday world, and both experiences result in an epiphany. As part of this narrative, drugs and spirituality emerge as a dualism that punctuates the Coltrane biography and helps to explain the conception of *A Love Supreme*: Coltrane rids himself of social evils and finds inspiration from God. The artist's influences are transported away from the physical world, with its vices and corruption, to the metaphysical world, and, ultimately, the ground is prepared for Coltrane's spiritual journey and eventual deification. *A Love Supreme* is therefore perceived as a final stage in a process, a celebration of rebirth and renewal and his previous spiritual awakening.

The deeply autobiographical nature of *A Love Supreme* invites the listener to directly relate the musical narrative to Coltrane's life experiences. Although Coltrane was no stranger to creating works that had a personal or social dimension—consider works that are dedicated to friends and family (*Naima, Cousin Mary, Mr. P.C., Syeeda's Song Flute*) or to more overtly spiritual or political themes (such as *Alabama* or *The Reverend King*)—within the context of *A Love Supreme*, the personal becomes all the more intense and profound. From the supporting liner notes to the *A Love Supreme* poem or "Psalm"—a personal celebration of Coltrane's devotion to God—which are both written by Coltrane, personalized interpretations of the work are encouraged, especially when considering how unusual these writings are in the context of Coltrane's broader output. Indeed, Coltrane was often cited as being against the idea of liner notes, either encouraging his music to speak for itself or for the listener to approach each musical experience from his or her own perspective. As stated earlier, Coltrane's poem also forms the structure of the final movement of *A Love Supreme*, where the musical line mirrors the phraseology of his written text. As such, the movement is a musical manifestation of Coltrane's poem "spoken" through his saxophone.

The "drugs to divinity" binary in this context provides a very powerful motivation for the artist and a strong narrative for fans to latch on to. And yet, from 1965 to his death in 1967, Coltrane was certainly performing under the influence of LSD. Although we cannot determine the exact influence—either positive or negative—of heroin or LSD on artists and their music, the mere fact that Coltrane was experimenting with LSD at this stage is something that should warrant further discussion, considering both the problems and widespread documentation of his drug use in the 1950s. The majority of Coltrane writings fail to elaborate on this point or serve to play down the use of LSD: in other words, the move from heroin to LSD is not regarded as problematic—instead, there is a desire to portray Coltrane as clean and pure, regardless of the realities of the situation. Pausing on this for a second, the playing down of Coltrane's drug use in later life is a clear illustration of the way in which the Coltrane biography is controlled and manipulated to avoid criticism and contestation. Although we could argue that there is a significant difference between heroin as a depressant/opiate with highly addictive qualities and LSD as a hallucinogenic with mind-altering potential, there is no denying the significance of drug taking of any kind within a musical context—it does not seem appropriate to discuss heroin addiction in relation to music and then to ignore his use of LSD.

Medically, Lewis Porter stresses that Coltrane's use of LSD would not have contributed toward his decline in health; however, his use of LSD is still largely treated as a taboo when considering the grand narrative of the Coltrane life and legacy: consider, for example, why Porter's four reliable sources who inform him of Coltrane's use of LSD choose to remain off the record. To understand Coltrane as a drug user at the end of his life—regardless of type of substance—is perhaps a reality that musicians, cultish fans, and mythmakers alike would rather ignore because it rides against the grain of the heroic and spiritual jazz narrative. This is perhaps another reason why the release of *A Love Supreme* in 1965 represents Coltrane's magnum opus, arguably, with all releases following (and possibly including) *Ascension* relegated to Coltrane's problematic period and, potentially, influenced by LSD. And yet, the use of LSD is not only in line with the experimental spirit of the 1960s, it is also seen as a useful means of exploring alternate psychological states.

Paradoxically, Coltrane's drug use moves from acting as a barrier to spiritual awakening in the late 1950s, to becoming a pathway to spiritual awakening in the late 1960s—in other words, rather than charting a path away from drugs toward the divine, in the mid-1960s drugs provide Coltrane with some supposed access to the divine. As with the improvisation-composition binary mentioned earlier, the drugs–divine dichotomy can be neutralized, and these binaries do not necessarily have to be viewed in opposition. By using LSD, Coltrane moved closer to Eastern mysticism and embraced the spirit of experimentation at the time.

Although the late John Tchicai stated that he had not seen Coltrane take LSD, Tchicai discussed the way in which artists who experimented with LSD during this period would normally have to be ready to see the world in a completely new way, to understand connections between the physical and the metaphysical worlds. Tchicai suggested that this wasn't something that most ordinary artists could take on board successfully—you had to be ready both musically and philosophically.[31] With the use of a drug such as LSD, Coltrane could be carried beyond his physical being in a quest to become disembodied, fusing his sound with nature.

Live Jazz/Recorded Jazz: *A Love Supreme* and Disembodied Sound

With Coltrane, sound ruled over everything. It eventually superseded composition: his later records present one track after another of increasing similarity, in which the search for sound superseded solos and structure.[32]

The final jazz binary I want to explore concerns the relationship between recorded sound and live sound. Earlier, I discussed how studio recordings are often presented as events in themselves, live moments that are captured for eternity. And yet, despite the history of jazz often being aligned with a history of recordings, live jazz is still regarded as the primary means of experiencing the music. Within this context, the recording functions as a type of contradiction in the music, something that enables jazz to endure but barely captures the spirit of the moment. Writers, musicians, and audiences alike promote the idea of jazz as being at its most intense and profound when it is encountered in a live setting, with experiences of recordings not even coming close to the physical power of jazz when it is heard firsthand. Indeed, a measure of one's credibility as a jazz fan comes with accounts of having seen iconic jazz figures close up and in person. The sentiment "You had to be there" best summarizes this attitude, as musicians and writers recount stories of witnessing jazz in the making and the profound impact of coming into direct contact with the jazz greats.[33] The influence of recordings on the history of jazz has been the subject of several insightful writings in recent years.[34] However, although these perspectives seek to redress the balance and acknowledge the primacy of recordings in readings of jazz history, the notion that recordings play a secondary role to live performance remains largely intact within broader jazz discourse. I have been interested to explore ways in which the dominance of the live performance over experiences of recorded jazz can be challenged, especially when listeners encounter iconic recordings such as *A Love Supreme*.

This is from Evan Eisenberg's seminal text, *The Recording Angel*: "Any new art, but especially one that is also a new medium, relying on technology to bridge distances in space and time, needs icons. For if the audience is being given something, it is also being deprived of something: a human presence."[35] Eisenberg comments on the way in which the limitations of recording technology, the removal of the physical body from the reception of music, results in compensatory gestures, namely the establishment of iconic personalities who convey meaning through sound. The denial of the human presence of an artist would usually result in music being perceived as inferior or as an obvious form of mechanical reproduction. And yet, when recordings are made by iconic artists, they take on a different mode of existence. In Coltrane's case, a recording such as *A Love Supreme* can become more profound and meaningful when experienced *as* a recording. Indeed, as a studio creation, the *A Love Supreme* album dominates all other limited versions and experiences of Coltrane's suite. For example, although film documentation exists showing the Classic Quartet performing sections of the piece at the Antibes Juan les Pins Festival in 1965, and a full audio recording is available of the festival performance, the Impulse studio recording remains the acknowledged authoritative statement of Coltrane's initial conception.

And yet, to see the Classic Quartet performing the piece live is interesting as an act of witnessing. Indeed, to observe the physicality of performance, the interactions between musicians and the context within which they are playing, is invaluable to scholars and Coltrane fans alike. Although the Antibes performance is still a recording—either a complete live audio recording of the festival performance or an incomplete televised version of the first two parts of the performance—and thus not a replacement for the up-close and in-person experience, it would be easy to assume that, as audience members, we would get a better feel for the live performance of the Classic Quartet by digesting and analyzing this footage.

However, somewhat counterintuitively, I would argue that audiovisual evidence of the Classic Quartet performing in this context does not have the same impact on the listener when compared to the experience of Coltrane's studio album. Although the visual material (covering "Acknowledgement" and a large portion of "Resolution") and audio recording provide listeners with an alternative version of the suite, the Antibes Juan les Pins performance is rooted in an everyday context and resembles other extended footage of the quartet playing in European festival settings. Within the studio recording of A Love Supreme, the absence of the visual and the control of Coltrane's sound creates a context for music to be experienced as more profound and mysterious. In many ways, the album transcends its status as a physical object to become something more symbolic, a reified object and associated set of events that bring us closer to Coltrane's dialogue with God than any live performance could.[36]

The Antibes footage shows the quartet playing A Love Supreme on stage. However, after repeated viewings, it is possible to discern minor imperfections in the live performance and significant differences between the studio version and live performance. For example, the live version of the suite does not include Coltrane's strict iteration of his musical "Psalm," and throughout the performance the quartet play in a much more open-ended way, stretching the duration of the suite from about 33 minutes to over 45 minutes.[37] From the outset, we also become aware of issues of fidelity; the visual quality is not of a particular high resolution and the sound quality, including the balance of artists on stage and background noise from the audience, is far from ideal. Visually, we are also aware of the fact that this is a live event through the staging, the positioning of musicians, the festival setting, and the use of flash photography. Ironically, although this is a live performance that has been documented audiovisually, it somehow feels more staged than the studio-based recording and we are more conscious of the way in which the music is mediated. Not only does the microphone visibly stand between us and Coltrane but we also become acutely aware that someone else is framing our reading of the music, simply by the way in which the performance is shot and the camera focuses on different members of the group.

Also, the fact that, when viewing the television footage, we are seeing the Classic Quartet as a low resolution black-and-white image affirms the status of the footage as a mediated act—it provides evidence of an event that, although happening in real time, feels somewhat distant and time-specific. In other words, just as we do not experience the world in black and white, it is difficult to experience a sense of liveness through an event that is clearly historic and fixed to a period in history.

Figure 1.6:
John Coltrane Quartet plays *A Love Supreme* in Antibes Jazz Festival in Juan-les-Pins, France, on July 26, 1965. Photo by Pierre Lapijover, courtesy of Yasuhiro "Fuji" Fujioka collection.

The Antibes footage also highlights the limitations of musical performance. We really do not have the opportunity to do a second take and have to accept the quartet as we find them. From the opening, we see Coltrane pausing following his opening cadenza, considering what to play. This observation alone is not a failing but something that draws us to the physicality and practicalities of performance; Coltrane *is* human, making conscious choices of what to play and what not to play. Even adulatory writers such as Ashley Kahn acknowledge the limitations of the Antibes performance, stating that "Coltrane assumed a traffic-cop role, cueing traditional passages and nudging the band along" and suggesting that "the surviving footage captures the performance losing focus as Garrison fumbles his cue to close the suite's first movement."[38] Kahn's words, although identifying minor mishaps, do not draw attention to other aspects of the performance that lack cohesion. For example, in contrast to the studio recording, Coltrane follows the opening cadenza with the *A Love Supreme* ostinato motif, laying down the feel for the band members to follow. And yet, when Jimmy Garrison enters, there is clearly some confusion about the feel and timing of the main motif as the bassist misses the rhythmic pickup to the *A Love Supreme* theme: in contrast to the studio recording, Garrison starts to play the *A Love Supreme* motif on the first beat of the bar as opposed to a quaver anacrusis that leads into the downbeat of the following bar. Again, these types of errors occur in live settings and are often exacerbated by the fact that other social factors, from background noise to reverberation, have an impact on musicians and their ability to hear each other. Coltrane himself went on record stating that outdoor events were not his preferred type of setting for the group and the work of the quartet was more suited to club settings.[39]

After a passage of what can only be described as musical negotiation between the group members, where the tempo and the *A Love Supreme* motif is bent and stretched, the players finally synchronize and Coltrane begins his solo. After listening to the Antibes concert on record for many years and only recently watching the surviving images of the event, I became aware of the way in which capturing performances visually tends to exacerbate the struggles of live performance. When watching Coltrane in Antibes, this straightforward point is evidenced in a couple of ways. First, as audience members, we become much more aware of the frailties and negotiations of performance when we watch jazz performances: in effect, it is much easier for us to pick up on mistakes visually than aurally as we see Coltrane gesturing, interacting with musicians, and so on. Second, the confusion in performance is mimicked through the way in which the television program is directed. The musical confusion is reinforced by the cuts between different camera angles, with images switching rapidly between Coltrane, Garrison, and Jones. It is as if, through the direction of the image itself, we are trying to gain some stability, some figure who will bind the performance together. Finally, these points add to the feeling of receiving the performance as a mediated image as we become acutely aware of others attempting to shape and frame our experience of the music. This point is reinforced when the musical performance gains stability, and occasional and rapid visual cuts away to Garrison and Jones disrupt the rhythm of the footage and the music, turning what is supposed to be the meditative Latin-based groove of "Acknowledgement" into an unpredictable and unsettling experience. In contrast to the studio recording, clearly Coltrane is not in control of his representation.

Presence and Performance

Although images of the Antibes concert can disrupt our experience of Coltrane and the Classic Quartet, showing them both as working musicians and mediated performers, experiencing the suite audiovisually can also feed into the mythic qualities of jazz, fueling our sense of the music as otherworldly or reinforcing the mystical presence of artists. Paradoxically, the separation of artists from their audiences by way of audiovisual media has the potential to instill music with a sense of mystery or romance. As Jed Rasula discusses the seductive menace of recordings in jazz history, I argue that the same can be said of visual representations of jazz.[40] For example, media producers such as filmmakers and photographers not only document performances but also feed into the construction of jazz itself; in effect, they frame music in such a way that it invites a particular reading or has connotative potential, their framing coming to stand for a whole series of cultural values.

With the Antibes performance, for example, the black-and-white imagery helps on the one hand to place jazz very much in the past, but on the other hand it takes it out of the ordinary and creates an environment for the music that is different from our everyday world, adding to the mystique of Coltrane's group. Despite the rapid camera cuts between individual musicians, the footage of "Acknowledgement" also includes a merging of images, blurring the shot of Coltrane (with Garrison in the background) with a shot of Elvin Jones's drumming hands. While this type of technique is common when used as a seamless movement between shots—fading one image out and introducing another—the Coltrane footage retains the superimposed camera angles for over seconds and then returns to the original camera angle of Coltrane and Garrison. The overall impact of this is that Coltrane takes on an almost ghostlike quality, the visual direction acting as an interpretation of the music.

The low-resolution quality of the images also, ironically, feeds the Coltrane mythology as we feel as though we are bearing witness to something we shouldn't be bearing witness to. This is exacerbated by the fact that the complete video of the performance remains unfound, either lost or in the hands of French television director Jean-Christophe Averty.[41] The lack of resolution and limited amount of footage fuels the voyeuristic tendencies and cultish behavior of jazz fans in a way similar to those of collectors who seek out rare recordings. The fact that the incomplete Antibes footage has only recently become widely available provides us with access to a rare and alternative world where *A Love Supreme* is available for us to see. I would suggest that visual representation is essential in the construction of iconic jazz musicians such as John Coltrane: visual representations not only enable us to make connections with iconic figures, but, by their very nature, the representations themselves can make significant contributions to artists becoming iconic in the first place.

These examples provide evidence of the way in which jazz recordings can move beyond the simple documentation of performances and the reproduction of live events toward broader cultural influence and related musical discourses. In other words, recordings have the potential to create what Mark Katz describes as the "phonograph effect," both responding to and shaping people's tastes, desires, needs, and aspirations.[42] With the studio recording of *A Love Supreme*, the absence of a physical presence feeds listeners' desires and helps to turn Coltrane and his music into mythic entities. There is a difference between Coltrane as a human being and Trane the myth, and the absence of body on record—and, by implication, the physical world—provides listeners with access to the idealized Trane.

In his study, "Free, Single, and Disengaged," for example, John Corbett describes the way in which the disembodied nature of recordings fuels a type of fetishistic audiophilia in listeners.[43] By their nature, recordings present consumers with a number of paradoxes that are mutually supportive. For example, they are simultaneously individualizing, developing intimate relationships between the listener and artist, *and* communalizing, encouraging individual consumers to feel part of a group. Furthermore, Corbett suggests that the lack of the physical presence on recordings results in the desire to fill the void created by the absence of body: we have a tendency to want to collect items and memorabilia that somehow connect us to the artist on record in order to fill the gap created by our disembodied experience. In other words, we long to get physically closer to artists and, therefore, consume records fetishistically in order to achieve this. Photographs, liner notes, and fan websites, for example, help us feel that we are somehow getting closer to the star and compensate for the lack of firsthand experience of the artist. My experience of Coltrane on video brings me closer to the artist, even if the experience is far from ideal. As a tactile experience, the album also engenders a type of fetishism that borders on the sensual: through the exploration of sound, the meticulous attention to detail, both in look and feel, and consumption of the gatefold release, consumers can feel physically closer to Coltrane.

Conversely, the void created by the absence of body on record leads us to a position where the artist is fetishized in an idealized state: we revel in the absence of physical presence and turn the recording into an idealized object that promotes the idea that music comes from the *beyond*, away from the physical world. Corbett states that "to render music free of noise is to grant it its proper musical status as sonically autonomous."[44] Here, the physical absence of artists is also reinforced by technology itself. By removing the scratching and hissing from recordings or creating equipment that hides the mechanical reproduction of music from view, the consumer can be encouraged to believe that music is somehow detached from the everyday world. Whereas in the past, the record was a tactile object that was penetrated by the stylus on a record player, in the CD age the disc is swallowed by the machine, and the mechanical reproduction of music is something hidden. I would argue that the growth of further digital formats takes the lack of physicality of recording to its ideal as we move toward an environment where we don't consume physical objects, and musical hardware is so small that it becomes inconsequential; we now experience music as if it can literally be plucked from the air. Within this context, listening spaces can be fetishized, and the experience of recordings can become bound up with a removal of oneself from time and place.[45] By treating the recording as a vehicle for an idealized experience, references to, and footage of, artists performing in the everyday world such as Coltrane playing at jazz festivals like Antibes ultimately leads to a sense of dissatisfaction, the practicalities and realities of music laid bare for all to see. Finally, as Eisenberg's earlier quote suggests, the lack of a human presence results in a need for icons, mythical figures who transcend their physicality and generate a unique and magical experience for listeners precisely through their absence. Coltrane's recorded sound becomes iconic; it has the ability to draw in listeners who forget that the material has been captured, edited, and mechanically reproduced.

Reactions to Coltrane's music, and the studio recording of *A Love Supreme* in particular, provide a good example of fetishistic audiophilia in action. The album encourages listeners to relate to Coltrane in physical terms through the consumption of the album's artwork, Coltrane's liner notes, poem and a backdrop that makes the recording the artist's most personal work. The album also encourages an idealized fetishistic response through the disembodied nature of the recording. In metaphysical terms, the album promotes a sense of mystery in the sonic experience fueled by an almost biblical creation myth and the spiritual dimension of the work. Coltrane's sound, the chanting of his voice, and the celebration of the recording as a unique sonic event also fuel the perception of the suite as an idealized experience. Overall, the album challenges the status and authority of jazz as a live-improvised art form and the recording as a mere documentation of performance. In other words, the live versus recorded music binary is disrupted and dismantled; while jazz is still widely celebrated as a live, improvised, and performative art form, the impact and influence of *A Love Supreme* is testament to the fact that the boundaries between the live and the recorded in music can be blurred. Indeed, the studio recording has a liveness that, ironically, is not captured in the Antibes event even though, as audience members, we can see the musicians on stage. The fetishistic nature of recorded experience can also lead to a position where recordings are felt as the primary, idealized jazz experience. When considering the influence and impact of iconic recordings such as *A Love Supreme*, I argue that jazz develops its most unique and powerful relationship with listeners at the moment the live performer is taken away.[46]

CONCLUSION

To conclude, *A Love Supreme* is an ideal iconic jazz work that can be used either to reinforce or to challenge existing jazz binaries. First, it is important to develop an understanding of why binaries exist, to explain the need for ideological control and the dominant discourse, ranging from the idealized construction of the jazz canon to the deification of Coltrane and his music. Where jazz is dominantly presented in binary terms, I suggest that these oppositions exist mainly as constructs that preserve an idealized view of jazz history that is devoid of complexity and contradiction. Neil Leonard's work *Jazz: Myth and Religion* describes the cultish behavior of jazz fans and the way in which the beliefs, rituals, and mythologies of music are preserved—binaries in this context can be used by a dominant social order to frame issues and to affirm beliefs, thereby maintaining order and control.[47]

Second, I would argue that we need to move beyond these forms of binary representation to resist a certain type of ideology. Essentially, canonical jazz works—namely recordings—can be viewed as multidimensional; if viewed in a certain way, they resist binary representations and challenge existing stereotypes. Contrary to straightforward musicological interpretations, *A Love Supreme* is successful because of its polysemy—the album has generated a multitude of meanings that appeal to different interest groups, and the album's musical and extramusical content combine to form a body of knowledge and influence. *A Love Supreme* moves beyond its physical status as a material object and turns into a monster trope; it becomes a symbolic code for everything "real" and authentic in jazz. Despite having a tangible and reified nature, the troping of *A Love Supreme* leads to the music appearing mysterious and impossible to define. The permanent recorded object confirms its status as a culture work that can be described, analyzed, and understood: it is a product of culture, and, simultaneously, it remains part of the processes of culture and continues to be invested with meaning to suit the needs of the present day. This double-edged nature, being both physical object and dynamic cultural signifier, is not unique to *A Love Supreme*, let alone jazz.

I would suggest that in moving beyond the binary, it is important to understand how oppositional distinctions between categories such as composition and improvisation have been articulated in particular settings. Further, our focus needs to be shifted away from an ontological assertion of difference and toward a more discursive view of binaries, and the way in which categories are used and modified in different settings. Through this type of approach, we can stress that in jazz, the use of the term "composition" (or composer), for example, is never neutral and inevitably feeds into politics and discourse. In effect, terms such as "jazz composition" and "improvisation," when inevitably treated in oppositional terms, imply that the characteristics that make live improvisatory practice distinct are also characteristics that make it superior to composed forms. As stated earlier, terminology is not innocent, and signs connote as much as they denote, and therefore use of these words in jazz is suggestive of particular value systems that underpin the music.

For example, the term" jazz composition" carries a range of different connotations. Whether we are exploring composition as a marker of jazz's canonical status or treating the concept as a mode of resistance to established performance practice or using the term to explore broader issues concerning art, gender, genius, race, collectivity, and so on, it is important to focus critically on the values assigned to jazz composition and improvised performance. By exploring what jazz composition means in certain settings, why it is demanded or why it is contrasted with improvisation, we can gain insights into particular groups, value systems, and the role that these concepts play in the creation of cultural identities. My discussion of Coltrane and *A Love Supreme* offers an example of this type of approach.

Coltrane's music beyond *A Love Supreme* did not clearly fall into simple oppositions and clear-cut categories. By thinking of music in a different way, we have an opportunity to challenge traditional, unreflective assumptions and mystifying statements that permeate jazz culture and, instead, engage with jazz composition as a complex and ideologically loaded practice. In asking why jazz is framed in antonymic terms, it is interesting to take an established canonical work and explore the way in which "jazzography," or the collected writings and representations of jazz, shape our understandings of the music. More than any other jazz album, *A Love Supreme* challenges the notion of binaries in jazz, and yet, paradoxically, the discourse surrounding the suite demonstrates the way in which binaries shape the history of jazz ideologically. Discussions and representations of *A Love Supreme* often weave a complex web of evidence to preserve the album's status as a canonical art, spiritual masterpiece, the magnum opus of jazz's greatest tenor man, a seminal recording, and one of the most groundbreaking works of the jazz tradition. *A Love Supreme* is symbolic in that it becomes a visual, aural, and tactile text for broader beliefs and mythologies, but it can also neutralize the mythic binaries of jazz and challenge established modes of musicological inquiry.

CHAPTER 2

From Reification to Deification

A Love Supreme *and the Canonization of Jazz*

We are living in a time of the rebirth of the gods, as a contemporary psychologist has put it, that is, a rebirth of the fundamental principles and symbols by which men live and by which the spirit of man survives.[1]

The religious poem and chanted refrain on John Coltrane's *A Love Supreme* served as a bridge between religious and secular music for some devout listeners who were generally mistrustful of the latter's social values.[2]

If anyone ever exhausted all the possibilities of running chord changes, he did. It just seemed that it was right for him to go cosmic, which he did.... He was God.[3]

Recordings play an integral role in the formation of a jazz canon, and they are the primary texts in asserting jazz's presence through time. Canons promote a sense of timelessness through enduring beauty and provide subsequent generations with a benchmark from which to measure their progress and achievements. In jazz, recordings have the ability to capture events that are located in history, evoking a clear sense of time and place. Yet, at the same time, they have the power to transcend the circumstances of their production: great recorded jazz can resonate with different audiences regardless of time and place. The consequences and politics of canonization have been widely discussed in jazz since the early 1990s, with a number of authors examining the impact of reification on jazz and the place of a canon within a newly constructed jazz tradition.[4] Jed Rasula, for example, describes the recording as a "seductive menace," using a paradoxical statement to sum up the impact not only of recordings but also of the canon itself.

Canons have incredibly seductive qualities as they enable people to celebrate what is perceived as the best a culture has to offer and also to learn from the masters of the past. There is no denying the power and influence of great jazz recordings on today's culture, from references to seminal recordings in film and literature to documentaries that tell the story of jazz. Even this book offers a clear indication of the value, impact, and influence of the jazz canon on society today. Canons also have a homogenizing role, supporting an infrastructure where the needs of critics, publishers, educators, and musicians can coexist and be mutually supportive. By agreeing on a body of works that are deemed valuable to all, the feeling of community can be galvanized and the canon can take on a naturalized form. Within this broader context, canons also serve to legitimate taste and authenticate experiences; having a body of great works to revere enhances a sense of tradition and promotes a degree of cultural continuity, where we are encouraged to believe that times change but our essential values remain intact. Canonical works do move from one generation to the next, giving the impression that they have stood the test of time—but the notion of works having inherent value can be challenged head-on. Indeed, the value and meanings associated with canonical works changes and adapts from context to context and from one generation to the next, as new meanings continually accrue. Part of the seduction of the canon is its ability to present the values of the present day as natural and timeless, as if great creative work has always been perceived and understood in the same way. Canons can be understood as deeply political and ideologically motivated, their inevitability, power, and influence seeming all-encompassing and their values perpetuating assumptions about great art being divorced from society. While canons are inevitable—and provide a backdrop to any art form that has claims to a degree of cultural worth—they are based on exclusion, reflecting only limited examples of cultural works and outputs.

Whether it is on the grounds of race, gender, class, or geography, canons typically foreground the work and values of a particular social group or elite at the expense of others, suggesting that genius and creativity are the domains of a select few. Sherrie Tucker, for example, has written extensively on the way in which canons exclude women from jazz history either by creating social obstacles, ignoring or downplaying female contributions to jazz or rewriting histories to favor a narrative of "great men."[5] More subtly, canons also encourage singular readings of works, placing emphasis on creative individuals as sole creators. Within a jazz context, this often means that individual artistry is revered at the expense of creative collaboration and the history of the music more frequently revolves around a set of iconic personalities, a pantheon of gods, or a metaphorical Mount Rushmore of jazz. Genius figures who create an enduring legacy of jazz works are often presented as conduits for divine inspiration, their works touched by God. Within this context, canonical art is perceived as autonomous, existing outside the influence of the social or everyday world, even though the circumstances of its production stem from everyday experience. In being represented as autonomous, great jazz recordings can transcend their social circumstances, being perceived as existing outside the influence of the commercial recording industry. Indeed, part of the seduction of a canon of great art is its ability to appeal to, and reflect, the values of cultural elites and to promote the idea that music can "speak for itself." What is promoted as "good for you" might not necessarily tally with what is popular, so advocates of the jazz canon would not be troubled by a separation of the music from the broader influences of popular culture. In effect, the canon exerts an influence that suggests masterworks must be consumed, owned, and revered even if the works themselves do not sit well with popular taste. Indeed, high-profile jazz advocates such as Wynton Marsalis have famously gone on record to challenge the value of popular taste and the whims of popular culture by suggesting that the pursuit of jazz can literally move us to "higher ground."[6]

Paradoxically, the jazz canon sidesteps the fact that jazz recordings are commodities, products that are designed to be bought and sold, and plays down the importance of commercial forces. Indeed, only when the narrative suits are sales figures used to support an album's quality, as if commercial success is an indicator of aesthetic quality. For example, Miles Davis's *Kind of Blue* is often revered for its commercial success, as if record sales are testament to the album's enduring aesthetic significance. When the positive endorsements of *Kind of Blue* are compared to criticisms of Miles Davis's later work, the issue of commercial success, record sales, and the music's position within the commercial marketplace are used as indicators of the music's failure; Davis's later works are presented as noncanonical, with Davis essentially being described a "sellout." Canons serve to create a binary between art and commerce, but in reality this distinction acts as a smokescreen for certain values and tastes to pervade.

A LOVE SUPREME AS CANONICAL WORK

Perhaps more than any other jazz album, *A Love Supreme* has come to stand as a centerpiece of the jazz canon: its centrality both to the output of John Coltrane specifically, and to jazz history more broadly, remains unquestioned. *A Love Supreme* has a symbolic quality that feeds into several jazz mythologies, supporting the sense of homogenous tradition, canon, and spiritual jazz life. The continued success and symbolic appeal of *A Love Supreme* has been made more significant in the context of the widespread adoption of what DeVeaux described as the "official jazz history," the promotion of a homogenous tradition born out of African American experience.[7] Although I would suggest that the notion of a singular jazz tradition can be viewed as a monolithic construct that serves an ideological function within society, the celebration of stylistic change, key players and masterworks, and a teleological narrative offers an attractive model from which to understand jazz history. The mere fact that we label the album John Coltrane's *A Love Supreme*—not the Classic Quartet's *A Love Supreme*; or John Coltrane, Bob Thiele, and Rudy Van Gelder's *A Love Supreme*; or Impulse's *A Love Supreme*—is already suggestive of a particular ideological viewpoint: one that not only reflects copyright law and the legal structures that shape the industry but also understands musical genius as rooted in the individual and promotes great music, perhaps, as autonomous and devoid of social influence. More than any other jazz album, *A Love Supreme* invites this singular reading, as the album has become so integrally bound up with John Coltrane's quest for spiritual discovery and unqualified devotion to God: it is the most personal of his jazz compositions. And yet the album has moved far beyond the personal toward something iconic, existing beyond the boundaries of a purely sonic document. The official history of jazz has had an interesting and ideologically loaded impact on the representation of Coltrane and his works, with the majority of writings and biographies creating a teleological narrative that reaches its pinnacle with *A Love Supreme*.

The canon works in mutual support of the jazz tradition: its sense of timelessness and enduring quality not only gives the impression that values are rooted in the past but also provides jazz history with a sense of evolution and continuity. The linear narrative bound up with the dominant jazz history is also supportive of the canonical ideal, as neat 10-year periods are each crowned with their own set of genius figures and masterworks to celebrate. Equally, by promoting each stylistic period as taking jazz to a new creative level, an evolutionary and teleological history is constructed. The suggestion that one generation builds on the work of the next leads us to a position where we regard each release as being informed by what had gone on before (hence, is better) and that a musician's work inevitably improves with age. Teleological narration is a key tenet of the official history of jazz and is underpinned by the division of jazz history into a succession of 10-year movements.

However, the contradictions begin to arise when we follow the teleological narrative to its logical conclusion, namely that if each musical work builds on the successes of the previous generation, then each artist's final work should represent his magnum opus and the evolutionary pinnacle of jazz musicianship should be found in the present. Within a scientific context, the notion that progress and evolution culminate in the expertise of the present is well established (if not necessarily accurate), and yet, within jazz, where historic recordings such as *A Love Supreme* are concerned, there is an overriding feeling that nothing in the present can compete with the iconic performances of the past. This is where the conflict lies within the official history of jazz: teleological and causal narratives are celebrated and championed to the point where they assert the authority of the underlying principles of the jazz mainstream; however, they immediately fall to pieces when used as a means of explaining the progress and development of jazz outputs to the present day. These contradictions apply within the narrative of artist biographies themselves. For Coltrane, the notion of *A Love Supreme* as the pinnacle of his achievement comes into conflict with the teleological narrative and calls into question the value of music post–*A Love Supreme*.

Within the dominant Coltrane narrative, an evolutionary pattern occurs where formative experiences and his professional years culminate in the production of *A Love Supreme*. Thematically, the story moves from the devoted student to musical apprentice in the navy, rhythm and blues showman to talented artist (albeit with a drug problem). This narrative trajectory, moving from student to master and from utility and commerce to art, is familiar and relates more broadly to the themes of jazz discourse. However, *A Love Supreme* demonstrates a move beyond the status of artist to become a divinely inspired conduit through which God speaks. The teleological narrative that underpins both the dominant jazz history and the supporting biographies of artists such as Coltrane is problematic, especially when dealing with historical periods that are fraught with complexity and contradiction. The linear history of jazz typically reaches a crisis position toward the mid-1960s as uniform jazz styles and the promotion of a homogenous tradition become difficult concepts to retain. In many respects, artists such as Coltrane were responsible for opening up jazz to different influences and challenging the assumptions upon which the tradition was founded until that point. Coltrane's fascination with musics from around the world and his experiments with "the New Thing" led to a far more open-ended model of music making.

And yet, within the context of Coltrane's biography, the extremities of these activities—and Coltrane's willingness to move beyond the fairly narrowly defined concept of the jazz tradition—resulted in his music being both divided into specific developmental periods explained away through biographical detail. When dominant jazz histories portray a crisis period from the mid-1960s, where the uniform nature of jazz is challenged, so too does the Coltrane story. Indeed, *A Love Supreme* occupies a distinct place within the artist's career, appearing as the culmination of Coltrane's work from the late 1950s to the mid-1960s. As Ekkehard Jost states, "Musically, *A Love Supreme* is the consummate product of an assimilation process in which Coltrane sums up five years of musical experiences and perceptions. As such, it achieves a synthesis of the most varied formative principles."[8] Jost feeds into the unity and synthesis narrative, arguing that *A Love Supreme* represented the culmination of work that Coltrane had undertaken previously. Therefore, the album has been portrayed as embodying unity both internally and externally.

This internal unity is evidenced through Lewis Porter's thematic and formal analysis, which demonstrates the way in which the suite ties together with a cell structure that is founded on the same pentatonic principles. Equally, the form of the album is given unity by its supposedly symmetrical nature. Externally, the theme of unity ties into Coltrane's development as a musician: *A Love Supreme* assimilates all that has been worked on previously, and is the synthesis of Coltrane's invention and ideas up until that point. And yet, as Ben Ratliff suggests, the album moves beyond a mere summation of what has gone before. *A Love Supreme* fulfills the romantic ideal of the artist's magnum opus: "It is not just another cusp in a series of cusps but the fulcrum of his career, setting the outline understanding both his past and future work."[9]

In viewing the album in this way, the reading and understanding of Coltrane's work post–*A Love Supreme* becomes difficult to envisage. Once the master has created his magnum opus, what is the status of subsequent works? The romantic ideals of other teleological histories and artist biographies often suggest that an artist's final works are the most spiritually profound and meaningful.[10] While *A Love Supreme* serves the narrative purpose of having all the traits of a last work, there are obviously a number of significant recordings which followed this seminal album.[11] It is as if works post–*A Love Supreme* are divorced from the iconic Coltrane: they sit uncomfortably within the romance of the jazz tradition and do not fit with the ideal of his magnum opus being the most sacred, special, and final work. On the whole, Coltrane's later pieces are recognized more as experiments, jazz as process rather than as polished product, and the later music is rooted more in the social context of the mid-1960s than the timeless space of canonical arts. A boundary exists, therefore, between Coltrane's work up to and including *A Love Supreme*, and beyond *A Love Supreme*.

Coltrane's recorded work after 1964 is problematic for a number of reasons. As previously stated, even though the album is not Coltrane's last work, it does carry with it all the trappings of an artist's last work. From the dialogue with the divine to being presented as the culmination of a journey, the end of a teleological period of evolution, the romance of *A Love Supreme* produces a sense of narrative closure that is played out in several ways, regardless of where the album appears in Coltrane's output. First, *A Love Supreme* appears as the culmination of the work of the Classic Quartet in unadulterated form. Although Archie Shepp and Art Davis appeared as part of the recording session, their absence from the final recording preserves the sanctity of the album and the uniformity of the Classic Quartet. Subsequent studio recordings of the Classic Quartet appear to serve either as postscripts to *A Love Supreme*, as posthumous releases, or as projects that mark the expansion (and dissolution) of the group.

Second, *A Love Supreme* marks the end of a physical quest: Coltrane's devotion to God and sense of spiritual purpose manifests itself in his receiving the album physically. Subsequent works move beyond the physical toward the metaphysical. It is as if a new Coltrane has to be invented following the production of *A Love Supreme*, a complete artist who has now transcended the everyday world and occupies a type of transcendental space.[12] This ties into David Ake's analysis of the changing musical persona of Coltrane, where the icon's musical style is discussed as either a form of "being," "becoming," or "transcendent." Ake describes the way in which Coltrane's career moves through these transitory states and how these concepts serve to frame the mythic representations of Trane.[13] I would argue that *A Love Supreme* provides a model for moving the Coltrane persona away from a state of "becoming" toward the "transcendent." In other words, *A Love Supreme* has a symbolic Janus-like quality in that it marks the end of Coltrane's physical pursuit and signals the beginning of his exploration of the metaphysical. If *A Love Supreme* is presented as a work in which Coltrane receives the word of God on earth—as Alice Coltrane suggests—then subsequent works signal an inversion of this process, moving Coltrane away from receiving the spirit to entering the spiritual realm itself. Even album titles released in Coltrane's lifetime such as *Om* and *Ascension* promote this ideal: ascension, for example, being the multifaith concept that describes the rare occasions when special individuals have the opportunity to ascend into heaven without dying. By stressing the religious concept of returning the body to heaven (or entering heaven alive), Coltrane feeds into a plurality of spiritual influences and serves to reinforce the idea that his music has entered a higher plane. Indeed, the majority of albums post–*A Love Supreme* feed into the universal spiritualism promoted by Coltrane throughout the mid-late 1960s. As his magnum opus, *A Love Supreme* can be understood as marking, mythically, the death of Coltrane as inspired by the physical world; unlike other artists or romantic genius figures whose final works are cut short by death or touched by the divine, Coltrane has the opportunity to interact with gods, entering the spirit realm without forsaking the body. Coltrane's movement from the physical to the metaphysical world has mythical and mystical associations: through stories of his transcendence and saintly qualities, Coltrane is presented either as a Christ-like figure or a modern-day Orpheus.[14]

Third, *A Love Supreme* can also be understood as the last great work of Coltrane's that shares a common language and structure with the established tradition. Blues forms and phrases form an integral part of the structure of the work, and, even though the album is presented as a suite, there are still clear references to standard forms.[15] Later Coltrane recordings are often perceived as uncontrolled or wildly free in nature, and the nonteleological nature of Coltrane's musical sound occupies an uncomfortable place within the official history of jazz, especially given Coltrane's bebop pedigree.

Fourth, and allied to the previous point, the addition of young musicians without proven pedigree and with black nationalist political agendas became a regular occurrence following the recording of *A Love Supreme*. The inclusion and embracing of musicians without a proven track record and questionable musical credentials and political attitudes rides against the developing jazz aesthetic of the master musician, the singular heroic virtuoso who can cut people off the stage.

Finally, as discussed in the previous chapter, Coltrane's alleged use of LSD from 1965 onward is something that is difficult for writers and fans working within the boundaries of canonical jazz history to deal with; within this setting, *A Love Supreme* provides a clear and unproblematic assertion of the drugs versus divine binary. The ideological control of the Coltrane narrative is perhaps more subtle than excluding the late works from Coltrane's biography. Instead of ignoring Coltrane's subsequent output and the move to more free-form and experimental projects, there is a need to reassert *A Love Supreme* as the final or most meaningful work that all his other works relate to in some way. The symbolic importance of *A Love Supreme* is certainly enhanced by the circumstances of the time and the development of spiritual and tran-scendent themes. The impact of *A Love Supreme* is also strongly increased with the benefit of hindsight, and feeds into the notion of history being written in retrospect. Jost continues: "It is doubtful whether the same piece, under a different title and without Coltrane's religious confession on the record jacket, would have attracted the kind of attention it ulti-mately did."[16] Indeed, it could be argued that *A Love Supreme* would not have developed into such a symbolic offering had Coltrane not died in 1967. Arguably, the premature death of the artist created a position where the musical output of Coltrane was recalibrated to demonstrate a logical and seemingly unified set of musical releases, as well as a clear developmental trajectory. Coltrane's death certainly contributed to the success and symbolic qualities of *A Love Supreme*, alongside a reasser-tion of the mainstream agenda that downplayed the later works as less significant or, indeed, as a necessary departure for Coltrane once the conventions of jazz had been taken to their creative limits. As Frank Kofsky argued, the death of Coltrane (and, indeed Albert Ayler) not only deprived the avant-garde of a much needed leadership in the 1970s but it also provided jazz traditionalists with the incentive to reclaim control of the discourse and, subsequently, appropriate the Coltrane legacy for their own purposes.[17]

MEDIATING COLTRANE

A Love Supreme is widely understood and promoted as Coltrane's most personal work. The album is not only perceived as difficult to imitate—considering how personal the suite is to Coltrane's life or, as Ravi Coltrane argues, the fact that the album goes beyond the musical to something sacred—but the work is also presented as a form of unmedi-ated expression.[18] This is obviously a paradox to begin: any studio album is by definition a product of mediation. Significantly, the lack of perfor-mances of *A Love Supreme* following its recording demonstrates the way in which the album has a unique place within Coltrane's output. Despite this, the album as a mediated object does not interfere with the promo-tion of *A Love Supreme* as an unadulterated statement of Coltrane's personal quest. When comparing the *A Love Supreme* story to broader Coltrane discourse, there are surprising changes in approach to the issue of mediation.

For example, the influence of Coltrane's recording company, Impulse, is often cited as the main reason for the artist recording a series of audience-friendly albums between 1962 and 1963.[19] Three albums in particular—*Ballads, Duke Ellington and John Coltrane,* and *John Coltrane and Johnny Hartman*—are interpreted as projects that were designed to appeal to a wider audience and to reestablish Coltrane's popularity with audiences following his perceived departure into more experimental forms. Because the albums were more overtly targeted at a wider audience and involved limiting the amount of extended improvisations, several commentators suggest that these projects were born out of pressure from Bob Thiele and Impulse in order to appease jazz critics who had reacted badly to Coltrane's extended improvisations and collaborations with musicians such as Eric Dolphy.[20] As Ben Ratliff suggests, *Ballads* was a contrivance between Coltrane and Thiele—something Coltrane was prepared to "give himself over to"—again, casting Coltrane as the manipulated subject ceding power and influence to his record company. Ratliff goes on to suggest that although Coltrane chose the repertoire for *Ballads* himself, the fact that he did not perform the material again in a live setting demonstrates the fact that the album was not of central importance to the artist (and, by implication, proves that it was the brainchild of Impulse and not Coltrane).[21]

Just because material is not performed again in a live setting should not necessarily mean that the music presented is not significant or meaningful to the artist concerned. Indeed, this conclusion is problematic especially when applying the same logic to *A Love Supreme.* The irony here is that because *A Love Supreme* is treated as a unique "event," it does not demand to be played again. Indeed, although it is interesting historically to hear and see the Classic Quartet performing *A Love Supreme* in Antibes in 1965, the concert is arguably seen as a distraction, a poor representation of Coltrane's vision and something that, had the circumstances been different, Coltrane would not have performed. With the *Ballads* album, on the other hand, because the tracks are popular songs, there is a demand and expectation for the music to be played over and over. These conclusions again demonstrate the way in which Coltrane's music is falsely divided between popular and artistic pursuits.

Within canonical accounts of jazz history, the presence of record companies and their commercial imperatives are never discussed in any critical detail. Paradoxically, even though canons can be seen as antithetical to the commercial recording industry, the canonicity of *A Love Supreme* is reinforced by commercial factors, not only in that it demonstrates the album's enduring success among different generations of listeners but also in relation to the number of units sold. Unlike other seminal jazz albums, however, in which sales units are carefully measured and used to endorse the status of the product, *A Love Supreme*'s commercial existence also carries with it a degree of mystery: the exact number of recordings sold remains an estimate. In an interview with Ashley Kahn, Michael Kauffman, the senior vice president at Verve records stated: "There were complexities between the sales reporting systems of the various companies that owned the music over the years. Sometimes the data was hard to find, or to merge, or maybe even it dropped out."[22]

Although Kahn expresses regret that *A Love Supreme* was not given the industry accolades it deserved (gold discs, platinum discs, etc.), I would argue that the ambiguity of sales figures supports the album's canonical and spiritual status: we know the album has reached many people but the number is probably much larger than we could imagine. Within a broader context, canons serve to establish a gulf between art and commerce that does not exist in reality. In fact, as an examination of the jazz canon would demonstrate, its masterworks are also all champions of the marketplace and are produced within the cut and thrust of the commercial recording industry. In the presentation of Coltrane the artist, there is a tendency to portray him as both immune and uninterested in the trappings of the commercial recording industry.[23]

The view of Coltrane as manipulated subject does not correspond with accounts of the artist's standing and influence at Impulse records. Indeed, as Lewis Porter noted, "Coltrane was given complete artistic control, even over the packaging of the LPs. The contract was renewed in April 1964, raising his yearly advance to twenty-five thousand dollars. Coltrane was financially successful, and he stayed with Impulse from then on."[24] The shifting presentation of Coltrane as either exploited subject who was under pressure from his recording company or as autonomous recording artist who had total control of his representation at Impulse clearly serves to resolve any problems or political conflicts within the Coltrane biography and feeds into underlying myths about great jazz being divorced from industry. As the canonical jazz tradition perpetuates false distinctions between art and commerce, there is a strong need to separate Coltrane's popular products from the more art-based pursuits. When *A Love Supreme* is discussed, Coltrane is placed at the center of the creative process: the album is entirely his conception prior to, during, and after the recording session. Both Bob Thiele and Rudy van Gelder are cast in a supporting or subservient role to avoid the impression that the album has been produced or engineered, and, unusually for his recorded legacy to date, Coltrane was instrumental in putting together the liner notes and selecting the photograph that was to appear on the album's cover. All of these strategies serve to limit the amount of mediating influences and show how the album is entirely the product of Coltrane's genius.

In the previous chapter, I stressed how a sense of liveness was important to authenticate the album's place within the jazz canon, and yet, this observation feeds into a much bigger question of how *A Love Supreme* is portrayed as a form of unmediated expression. By drawing attention to outtakes, alternative versions, changes in personnel, overdubbing, engineering setup, and production, it is easy to get a feel for the complexity of the recording process and the variety of mediating roles involved in putting an album together. To describe *A Love Supreme* solely as a product of Coltrane's creativity or personal quest and to suggest that the artist had no interest in the potential marketplace for this project both seem like significantly misconceived and romanticized statements, especially considering how the design of the album is calculated to build on—and feed off—Impulse's existing catalogue. In view of the way in which Coltrane's involvement with Impulse records is discussed, moving from accounts of Coltrane being "forced" into performing certain types of repertoire to having complete control over his artistic outputs, we get a clear sense of how the Coltrane narrative is changed and adapted to support underlying values and mythologies. For example, when the album is regarded as an artistic or spiritual success, then the music is unmediated, created outside the control of the record company. When the music is more "commercial" in orientation, then the recording company obviously dictated choices. In reality, these false distinctions can be seen as feeding into narratives about jazz and its relationship to popular culture. Contrary to the shifting representation of Coltrane, we must assume that the artist had a tremendous influence at Impulse and therefore played an active part in constructing his public persona and choosing the types of material he performed. He would also have been aware of the commercial pressure of the marketplace and therefore worked with the company on the design, placement, and dissemination of his products.

Among other things, Impulse were instrumental in creating a particular aesthetic for jazz, championing the gatefold LP on all standard releases and developing a very distinctive marketing strategy that placed emphasis on fidelity, experimentation, vision, and honesty.[25] Impulse titles and album covers were specifically designed to reinforce the spiritual, political, or philosophical aspects of jazz and the label became heavily bound up with championing the New Thing.[26] In contrast to the design aesthetic of Blue Note and their use of monochrome photography, Impulse covers displayed a predominance of color both in terms of cover images, photographs, and the distinctive orange-and-black spine. These devices were also reinforced by the distinctive slogan "The New Wave of Jazz is on Impulse!" and the distinctive exclamation mark that follows the label's logo. With *A Love Supreme*, the Impulse design aesthetic was deliberately modified to single out the album as unique. For the first time in the label's history, the distinctive orange-and-black spine was changed to black and white as if to connote a sense of purity, difference, and timelessness.[27] The move to black-and-white design supported the spiritual theme of the album, as did the cover photograph, text, poem, and accompanying artwork, creating a different design aesthetic from the Impulse norm. The cover photograph (figure 2.1), taken by Bob Thiele, for example, shows Coltrane in a non-

Figure 2.1:
John Coltrane photo by Bob Thiele, courtesy of MaxJonesArchive@aol.com.

performative pose. The shot represents him in thought and in profile, looking slightly upward away from the camera. This image gives the impression that Coltrane is in a state of natural contemplation; as a piece of reportage, there is nothing staged, artificial, or posed about the photograph.

The album cover (figure 2.2) also features Coltrane in front of a set of railings that are placed upward diagonally from left to right. The angle of the railings is also paralleled by the use of text on the album cover, which is set out askew at the same angle as the railings, and also raised from left to right. While this technique places the cover in line with the codes and conventions of other jazz album covers, the angling of the text also subtly feeds into the spiritual theme of the album. By angling the text upward from left to right, the placement of the album title gives of a clear visual indication of ascendance. Coltrane's title is moving in an upward direction much as classical painting would display golden section principles. When coupled with the monochrome tones of the album, the cover image and title reinforce the underlying theme of the album itself.[28]

I have written previously on the use of monochrome photography in jazz and the way in which the technique serves to create a rich and complex set of associations for jazz.[29] Photographs provide a documentary role by capturing artists in the moment. However, by being presented in black and white, they also frame the music in such a way that it appears

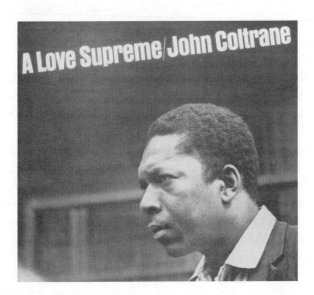

Figure 2.2:
John Coltrane's *A Love Supreme.*

immediately historical and, paradoxically, as existing outside history. Because viewers do not experience the world in black and white, monochrome photography has a mysterious dimension in which artists are transformed into appearing otherworldly. These images are powerful and vibrant and also serve to tap into feelings of nostalgia, purity, and honesty. Black-and-white images are also associated with photography as an artistic practice and, in many respects, monochrome shots demand to be taken seriously. I would therefore argue that the choice of the black-and-white image for the cover of *A Love Supreme* and design aesthetic is a significant feature in our reception of the album: even though the full connotative potential of monochrome photography might not have been discussed in the 1960s, the use of monochrome photography to frame jazz album covers as works of art in their own right was well established. The role that album covers play in framing music and its associated values is often overlooked. As Michael Jarrett states: "Record covers mirror back our perceptions of particular types of music, perceptions that are to a great extent visually and not musically determined.... Covers not only represent—encode in visual form—the myths associated with music, they contribute to the construction of those myths. They are part of the process that imbues music with meaning, giving it both a face and a voice."[30] The *A Love Supreme* cover has the ability to reinforce the values associated with the sounds of Coltrane and the Classic Quartet but can also serve to inform our reading of the music. The cover design has a timeless quality that exudes the qualities bound up with the album's conception and also fuels the broader mythic conceptions of *A Love Supreme* and Coltrane's changing transcendent representation.

In addition to the cover image, the gatefold release was also accompanied by Coltrane's *A Love Supreme* poem (or psalm), the title of which on more recent releases is given a gothic font as if to signify the sacred nature of the message, and a portrait of Coltrane drawn by Victor Kalim. The charcoal technique used by the artist in capturing Coltrane presents the artist as appearing out of the white backdrop of the cover itself, reminiscent of a church brass rubbing or religious shroud, and this, together with the liner notes, Coltrane's printed "Psalm," and cover design, supports the idea that Coltrane and spirituality go hand in hand (see figure 2.3). The text of Coltrane's "Psalm," *A Love Supreme*, is structured in a type of preacher-like prose, and James Hall's analysis of the poem underlines its rhetorical affinity to the language of the church. Coltrane combines extended passages with short statements and repeated words; one could easily imagine how the text could play out in

DEAR LISTENER:
ALL PRAISE BE TO GOD TO WHOM ALL PRAISE IS DUE.

Let us pursue Him in the righteous path. Yes it is true; "seek and ye shall find". Only through Him can we know the most wondrous bequeathal.

During the year 1957, I experienced, by the grace of God, a spiritual awakening which was to lead me to a richer, fuller, more productive life. At that time, in gratitude, I humbly asked to be given the means and privilege to make others happy through music. I feel this has been granted through His grace. ALL PRAISE TO GOD.

As time and events moved on, a period of irresolution did prevail. I entered into a phase which was contradictory to the pledge and away from the esteemed path; but thankfully, now and again through the unerring and merciful hand of God, I do perceive and have been duly re-informed of His OMNIPOTENCE, and of our need for, and dependence on Him. At this time I would like to tell you that No MATTER WHAT . . . IT IS WITH GOD. HE IS GRACIOUS AND MERCIFUL. HIS WAY IS IN LOVE, THROUGH WHICH WE ALL ARE. IT IS TRULY—A LOVE SUPREME—.

This album is a humble offering to Him. An attempt to say "THANK YOU GOD" through our work, even as we do in our hearts and with our tongues. May He help and strengthen all men in every good endeavor.

The music herein is presented in four parts. The first is entitled "ACKNOWLEDGEMENT", the second, "RESOLUTION", the third, "PURSUANCE", and the fourth and last part is a musical narration of the theme, "A LOVE SUPREME" which is written in the context; it is entitled 'PSALM'.

In closing, I would like to thank the musicians who have contributed their much appreciated talents to the making of this album and all previous engagements.

To Elvin, James and McCoy, I would like to thank you for that which you give each time you perform on your instruments. Also, to Archie Shepp (tenor saxin) and to Art Davis (bassist) who both recorded on a track that regrettably will not be released at this time; my deepest appreciation for your work in music past and present. In the near future, I hope that we will be able to further the work that was started here.

Thanks to producer Bob Thiele; to recording engineer, Rudy Van Gelder; and the staff of ABC-Paramount records. Our appreciation and thanks to all people of good will and good works the world over, for in the bank of life is not good that in-vestment which surely pays the highest and most cherished dividends.

May we never forget that in the sunshine of our lives, through the storm and after the rain—it is all with God—in all ways and forever.

ALL PRAISE TO GOD.

With love to all, I thank you,

John Coltrane

impulse!
Mono—A-77
Stereo—AS-77
MADE IN U.S.A

Figure 2.3:
Victor Kalim's sketch of John Coltrane from the inside cover of *A Love Supreme*.

a religious setting with punctuating statements such as "Thank you, God" appearing 11 times, almost like a response to a preacher's call.[31]

The mediation (and mediatization) of Coltrane is a complex subject that strikes to the heart of the artist's representation and development as a cultural icon. Although it is tempting to view Coltrane as an artist untainted by the demands of a changing recording industry or, indeed, as a musician who used technology only to passively document his music in an unadulterated fashion, the complex reality of the situation is that Coltrane clearly had an awareness of his representation, the changing marketplace for his music, and the potential of recording tech-nology to enhance his sound. By continuing to present Coltrane and his music as unmediated, it is easy to fall into the romance of feeling that he is speaking directly to the listener, that only music mattered to him and that, as an artist, he was not concerned with either the politics of his time or the commercial potential of his music. By viewing Coltrane in this way, it is very easy to imagine that we can experience the "real" Coltrane, unlike present-day celebrities who are media constructs, engineered personalities who are born out of formulaic types of representation.[32] To imagine that there is a type of Coltrane brand or specific strategy of representation would appear at odds with the tropes of honesty and integrity bound up with the musician and his music.

While I am not claiming that Coltrane was lacking honesty and integrity, I am suggesting that the mediation and mediatization of Coltrane play a central role in our reception of the artist, both during his lifetime and beyond. When Coltrane's obsessive practices are described, from his endless stamina and practice routines to anecdotes of him falling asleep with his saxophone in his mouth, from his monumental improvised performances to stories of him filing down his teeth down in order to achieve a better quality sound, all other aspects of his life are downplayed: *music* is all that matters. The Coltrane narrative presents jazz as an all-or-nothing pursuit, an unmediated form of expression that lies beyond the influence of the social or everyday world.[33]

This mirrors the work of Philip Auslander, whose book *Liveness: Performance in a Mediatized World* challenged many of the mythologies associated with performance practice and the reverence of artists. Auslander examines the value of liveness in the arts and the desire to regard performance as a form of unmediated expression. His work questions many of the assumptions about the differences between the live and the mediatized and stresses that all works, whether considered live or recorded, are mediated in some way; as such, most forms of performance are affected by mediatization in some way. Auslander argues that concepts such as the live and the mediatized (recorded, televised, etc.) have a value for performers and audiences alike but distinction between these concepts serves to produce another unhelpful binary opposition. Auslander seeks to challenge the common assumption that "the live event is 'real' and that mediatized events are secondary and somehow artificial reproductions of the real."[34] Auslander argues that previous distinctions between the live and the mediatized no longer hold true and, as live events are becoming ever more like mediatized ones, he questions whether there really are clear-cut ontological distinctions between the two types of event. Auslander's work echoes the writings of several jazz writers who have commented on the relationship between recordings and live performance, and his work seeks to deal with the dominance of mediatization on our culture, claiming that live events are now inevitably modeled on mediatized representations.[35]

From my perspective, albums such as *A Love Supreme* provide clear examples of a blurring of the boundary between the live-unmediated and mediatized-mediated. As stated in chapter 1, the liveness of Coltrane's studio album is often heralded, whereas live events such as the Antibes concert can be described as products of mediatization in that they are performed for a televised audience. Indeed, the musicians would obviously have been aware that their performance was part of a mediatized event, not only in that they performed onstage in front of microphones but also television cameras, as the concert was being filmed in front of a live festival audience. As viewers today, we can hear and see the concert only through audiovisual media and so are reliant on mediatization in order to experience this event.

Furthermore, although it is debatable how many audience members in Antibes would have heard Coltrane's *A Love Supreme* at the time of the Classic Quartet's performance in 1965, we also need to be aware of how live events are experienced as part of a mediatized culture. For example, Coltrane's audience would inevitably have had a series of expectations about the performance they were about to see based on their experience of Coltrane on record, in print, and in other contexts. The mediatized experience of *A Love Supreme* also explains why the Antibes concert does not compare favorably with the studio recording; it is inevitable that the Antibes concert will pale in comparison to the original recording, and repeated viewings will serve only to draw attention to issues of musical errors, sound quality, and so on. Despite the fact that all the existing versions of *A Love Supreme* are mediatized, the Coltrane narrative is frequently adapted in order to preserve a sense of distinction between the unmediated and the mediated.

DEIFYING COLTRANE

Since his death there has been considerable testimony to Trane's generous, almost saintly, nature. I believe it all.[36]

As enticing as the inevitable Trane/train metaphors may be, so are the Christ-like parallels. The saxophonist's life of self-sacrifice, message of universal love, death at an early age—even his initials—amplify the temptation.[37]

JOHN COLTRANE: In music, or—as a person... I would like to be a saint. [*John laughs, then Alice laughs*]
ENNOSUKE SAITO: You would like to be a saint, huh?
JOHN COLTRANE: [*laughs*] Definitely.[38]

Coltrane's statement about wanting to be remembered as a saint was given during his trip to Japan in 1966. Although at the time, Coltrane was expressing the desire to be the best person he could be in both musical and extramusical terms, the statement has taken on a greater significance following Coltrane's premature death in 1967. Today, treating Coltrane as a type of godly figure is no longer limited to cultish groups and fanatical supporters: both the artist and albums such as *A Love Supreme* are now firmly deified within broader jazz discourse. Indeed, Coltrane is revered spiritually and musically by a number of different groups, from musicians to audiences, biographers to journalists, and beyond. The simultaneous perception of Coltrane as a mediatized icon and as an unmediated artist serves to support Coltrane's deification as audiences are influenced both by the range of Coltrane materials, recordings, and ephemera available today, at the same time as feeling that they are receiving the message of the "true" Coltrane, an uncomplicated voice that exists outside the contrived and corrupt world of the commercial recording industry.

The view of Coltrane as a musician detached from his social environment is even reinforced by members of the Classic Quartet. McCoy Tyner, for example, has continually portrayed Coltrane as a spiritual leader with statements such as "John's first love was music—for him nothing else mattered."[39] This emphasizes the unmediated nature of Coltrane's work and serves to remove the artist from his contextual setting. The portrayal of Coltrane as an artist who produces pure music away from the influence of his surroundings was found before the tributes following the artist's death in 1967. Indeed, writers had been engaged in representing Coltrane in this way from the mid-1960s onward. For example, consider Joe Goldberg's appraisal of Coltrane's music after the release of *A Love Supreme* in 1965: "It is, as usual when a new idea strikes him, pure music, exhibiting a concern with notes and sound for their own sake."[40] Coltrane's artistry is described in autonomous terms; he is the creator of art for art's sake.

The idealized view of Coltrane as a type of unmediated artist is challenged head-on when romanticized accounts of his life and works are analyzed and deconstructed. For example, in several popular accounts of his life and music, Coltrane is described as unmediated on the one hand and as a type of medium, in and of himself, on the other. This type of narrative is evidenced through the discussion of Coltrane as a conduit through which God speaks, as well as an artist who is somehow connected spiritually and musically to past masters and ancient cultures. McCoy Tyner, for example, remarked that "John and Bird were really like messengers.... In other words, God still speaks to man."[41] Coltrane's seeming ability to converse with God raises his artistic status to that of a prophet, and he has subsequently been subjected to a range of different interpretations.

Following the artist's premature death in 1967, there has been a continual flow of anecdotes and theories that lay claim to mystical interpretations of Coltrane's last years or a sense of uneasiness about his conversance with God. Wayne Shorter, for example, described Coltrane's later performances in a fatalistic manner, as if the artist were aware of his impending death: "It's as if he were seeing the light—that grand light."[42] Further, pianist Bobby Timmons described the reaction of Coltrane's mother to the artist's spiritual awakening:

> I remember [John's mother] telling me about *A Love Supreme* and how she was wishing he'd never written it. I was surprised to hear her talking like that, but she told me John had a vision of God before he composed it...that he was seeing visions of God a lot of times when he was playing.... [S]he said, "When someone is seeing God, that means he's going to die."[43]

The range of stories about Coltrane's encounters with God provide an interesting backdrop to the range of spiritually inspired albums that followed *A Love Supreme*. As a suite composed in isolation and "received" from God, *A Love Supreme* provided the blueprint for subsequent works, which also served to cultivate the persona of Coltrane as being saintly and transcendent. The spiritual dimension of Coltrane's life and music and associated mythologies have triggered a number of comparisons to religious figures. Coltrane's persona is often compared to Christ or the Buddha, echoing the similar treatment given to Charlie Parker by beat poets but with a much greater intensity and diversity of followers.[44] Accounts describing Coltrane as a type of God range from facile comparisons such as the Ashley Kahn quote earlier, in which the initials "JC" call to mind Jesus Christ, to accounts of Coltrane having a saintly presence. Marion Brown describes an encounter with Coltrane: "I was playing this concert, and when I finished a solo, I backed off-stage. There was Coltrane with the lights behind him, beatified. He held out his arms and took me in and I wept like a child."[45] Coltrane's ability to reduce a fellow musician to tears demonstrates the way in which artists perceived his spiritual aura and saintly presence.

Furthermore, the perception of Coltrane as a type of medium or incarnation of God extended way beyond his immediate playing circle. In his influential work *Thinking in Jazz: the Infinite Art of Improvisation*,

Paul Berliner describes the impact that Coltrane's music has had on other musicians, creating a range of inexplicable feelings and responses. Describing the experience of a Japanese musician who was dealing with the death of his sister, Berliner states that, upon hearing Coltrane, the musician was "disarmed by the performance, he returned alone to his apartment and wept into the night. Rising at dawn from a restless sleep, he interpreted the experience as a sign that he was to become Coltrane's musical disciple."[46] Berliner's study describes the influence of artists such as Coltrane on different communities of listeners and discusses the impact Coltrane had on people both during his lifetime and, perhaps more significantly, following his death.[47] Coltrane's sound has obviously created several generations of imitators, and yet the spiritual dimension of his music has clearly had a much wider influence on listeners.

Musicians often go beyond the discussion of the technical aspects of playing to talk about the profound symbolic and emotional impact of Coltrane's music. In an article that explored the impact of Coltrane on British saxophonists in the 1990s, tenor player Alan Skidmore described the presence of Coltrane as mystical and inspiring: "I never set out to play like Trane, but the influence and inspiration is always there. No one else moves me the way he does.... He was driven by a spiritual force that most people don't understand."[48] Skidmore's words demonstrate how Coltrane's music has an influence beyond pure sound to the extent that it has now become bound up with feelings of sincerity, honesty, spirituality, and a sense of divine quest. Coltrane has an impact on musicians in ways that they themselves cannot comprehend.

These types of feelings are analyzed by Neil Leonard in his book *Jazz: Myth and Religion*, in which the growing significance of religion and spirituality in jazz are explored alongside the question of why jazz has increasingly been felt to be otherworldly. Borrowing from the work of Max Weber and Emile Durkheim, Leonard analyzes the role that myth and ritual plays in the establishment of jazz as a sacred practice. Although he does not suggest that jazz either is or isn't inherently sacred, Leonard's approach is more nuanced in seeking to understand why the music stimulates quasi-religious feelings and behavior in people. In discussing the work of Coltrane, Leonard describes the way in which Coltrane is perceived both as a medium through which God speaks, as well as a kind of shaman or prophet who can evoke ecstasy in people. Leonard uses musician Gerald McKeever's response to hearing Coltrane as an example of the way in which prophets can express thoughts and feelings in ways that everyday people can't, and articulate for the inarticulate: "I was sitting there, digging...screaming.... I *felt* so much of what he was saying, I had so much I wanted to say to the whole world...and *I didn't know how to get it out! He was my God!"*[49]

In a broader context, the portrayal of Coltrane as saintly or godlike is certainly reinforced by other narrative themes. For example, the perception of Coltrane as a type of medium extends beyond his godly influence to different artistic and musical contexts, to his being presented as a vehicle through which the African American tradition speaks. Indeed, writers and musicians have expressed the view that Coltrane not only was influenced musically by the work of past musicians but also that he maintained direct spiritual links to the masters of the past. An early biographer, O. C. Simpkins, for example, describes Coltrane as being guided by the spirit of Charlie Parker following a dream he had in which Bird came to encourage him to continue the work on his harmonic experiments. Simpkins describes the dream as a "visitation" and uses the anecdote as an explanation for Coltrane's subsequent work. For example, he states, "John would explain to McCoy many of his musical concepts...on which Charlie Parker had told him to continue working."[50] Within this context, there is the genuine belief that Coltrane was in communication with Parker from beyond the grave. Here, we have another take on the mediation of Coltrane and his music—Coltrane is the medium through which past icons of jazz speak to us; he is the embodiment of a living tradition. This anecdote is clearly blown out of proportion as if to demonstrate Coltrane's ability to converse with the masters of jazz history and to confirm his innate links to the African American past. While this approach could certainly be understood as problematic and overly romanticized, a product of uncritical scholarship, the currency and influence of Simpkins's work is present within recent studies of Coltrane's life and works that continue to promote the African American tradition as essential and mystical.[51]

By contrast, several writers have stressed the fact that Coltrane was not a natural-born genius: his successes were achieved by hard work, motivation, and continual searching. As Lewis Porter states,

> He was not, as one might have thought, a great talent who took a long time to get recognized. He was, rather, someone who did not begin with obvious exceptional talent, and that makes his case all the more interesting—one can become one of the great musicians of all time and not start off as some kind of prodigy.[52]

While the description of Coltrane's graft and craft might be perceived as lessening his claims to God-given status—he was not an innate genius—

Porter's words support the fact that his spiritual awakening and subsequent transformation is made all the more profound by his humble background, training, and work ethic. Indeed, his development as a musician helps to convey a type of ordinariness that supports the perception of Coltrane as unmediated—essentially, he is "one of us"—and yet, once touched by the divine, his transformation is made all the more remarkable as his music and continual searching take on a transcendent quality.

While Porter urges a sense of realism, stressing that Coltrane was not an isolated genius but a normal musician who developed as part of a creative group of musicians, the tendency of most writings on Coltrane's music is to promote a sense of divine inspiration or otherworldly quality. In addition to describing Coltrane's transcendent qualities, other biographers have sought to explain Coltrane's spiritual journey in fatalistic terms, as if his godlike status and tragic death were preordained. Bill Cole, for example, asserts that there is symbolic meaning in that Coltrane was born on a date when day and night were in perfect balance. Cole draws on the mysticism of astrology in order to heighten Coltrane's place within the cosmos and the sense of predetermination, his success written in the stars.[53] Cole also stresses Coltrane's innate links to Africa and finds ways of conflating Coltrane's music with religious themes and the spirituality of African cultures:

> It doesn't seem inconceivable to begin to relate the use of the triplet in his music to the symbolism of either the Trinity or the God-Man-Nature UNITY. The Trinity is clearly spelled out in the traditional religion of the Yoruba people of Nigeria. Olorun is the god-symbol; Eleda is the root form, the form from which all other forms are derived; and Ori is the communicator with the life-spirits on earth.[54]

Equally, other writers have used the strong influence of the black church in Coltrane's childhood to explain his later pursuance of spiritual themes, the Reverend Blair in particular providing a role model for Coltrane to emulate. More recently, even psychologists have suggested that Coltrane's continual searching can be understood as a reaction to the absence of father figures in Coltrane's life. Simplistically, Coltrane's obsessive character and continual desire for new perspectives can be understood as a type of void-filling activity.[55] These examples show that, regardless of the biographical interpretation, writers have a tendency to invest biographical details with symbolic meaning in order to explain the transcendent nature of Coltrane's music. Writings construct a totalizing narrative in which Coltrane's life is preordained, the speed of his development, premature death, and subsequent deification are treated as inevitable. Furthermore, Coltrane's own interest in cosmology and conceptions of spiritual awakening obviously aid this type of narrative, making his personal quest appear all the more natural and inevitable. The multitude of representations and mythologies of Coltrane leads to the artist being understood as the most saintly of jazz icons. The deification of Coltrane has therefore emerged from a confluence and development of narrative themes that distance the artist from the everyday jazz world.

Perhaps the most compelling example of Coltrane's deification comes in the work of the Saint John Coltrane African Orthodox Church, based in San Francisco, where Coltrane's music and writings are used as part a weekly liturgical service and community program. David Ake describes the use of Coltrane and his music within this religious context: "A painted icon of Coltrane (complete with halo) hangs above the altar, and church congregants venerate the saxophonist's recordings, particularly his works from *A Love Supreme* (1964) onward, as both that musician's own spiritual declarations and as aural sacraments for them to receive."[56] From this perspective, Coltrane's music transcends its status as jazz to something more profound. The transcendent qualities of Coltrane's late music provided the inspiration for the founding of the church, leading to him being received as a messenger: "Further investigation into this man proved him to be not just a 'jazz musician' but one who was chosen to guide souls back to God."[57]

Although several authors have sought to separate the living and breathing Coltrane from the mythic and transcendent Coltrane, or "Trane," as stated earlier, I argue that the interplay between these conceptions of real and mythic is more complex than simply focusing on the "music itself" as a way in to understanding the "real" Coltrane. The deification of Coltrane in everyday situations is seen most convincingly by the testimony of the people who knew him intimately or worked with him firsthand. Whether it is Alice Coltrane's use of biblical analogy to describe Coltrane's creativity or Ravi Coltrane's description of *A Love Supreme* as "sacred," Archie Shepp's description of Coltrane as Buddha or McCoy Tyner's description of Coltrane as a messenger from God, the fact that those closest to Coltrane have fueled the mythologies and deifying codes found in broader jazz discourse is significant. Indeed, these types of statement provide examples of how the formation of culture and identity is an iterative process, our relationships with people develop through the exchange of information through time, and the

Figure 2.4:
Saint John Coltrane African Orthodox Church in San Francisco, CA. Photo by Hiroki Fujioka, March 7, 2010, courtesy of Yasuhiro "Fuji" Fujioka collection.

continual renegotiation of our values and interests. Our relationship with people changes as we become influenced by the romance of broader discourse and develop selective and, at times, embellished memories about the deceased. This process is taken to the extreme when memories of John Coltrane are evoked, resulting in a continual focus on the saintly and a perpetuation of stories that inevitably create difficulties in separating the real from the mythic.

The impact of the Coltrane legacy provided a focus for a special issue of *Wire* magazine in 1991. As part of the responses to Coltrane's work, musician interviews, and retrospectives, writer Philip Watson expressed concern that the sacrosanctity of the Coltrane legacy was denying any degree of critical engagement with the subject. Watson sought to develop a critical perspective on the Coltrane legacy but stressed that the spiritual qualities of *A Love Supreme* in particular cannot be ignored:

> I've played a lot of records a lot of times, but I've played none as often as *A Love Supreme*. It's not a landmark record compositionally or improvisationally; its awesome power exists beyond the notes in what Cecil Taylor described as "a conception that goes way beyond that of his horn."

...THE PROBLEM is that because of these qualities Coltrane has almost become too colossal. It's easy to understand the obsession and elevation—whichever way you turn, technically, tonally or spiritually, Coltrane confronts you; never are the possibilities exhausted.[58]

Although, like other writers, Watson cannot ignore the power and symbolic nature of *A Love Supreme* and the impact it has had on listeners, he attempts to come to terms with the possible negative impact of the deification Coltrane and the influence of his legacy. First, he suggests that Coltrane's primary position as a revered icon has led to several generations of Coltrane imitators. This has, arguably, led the development of jazz up a narrow corridor. Second, he argues that the Coltrane legacy is limited and does not take into account the broader influences of Coltrane on experimental musicians. In effect, only the years 1959–1965 are celebrated and yet the Coltrane influence clearly extends beyond this period into other musical styles and art forms (this will be the focus of my next two chapters). Third, Watson suggests that it might be appropriate to treat Coltrane as an obsessive person, and draws on quotations from Miles Davis and James Lincoln Collier to document this. This mirrors the argument I make in *Jazz Icons*: that it can be fruitful to examine the complexity and contradictions of biography in order to engage critically with iconic figures. Finally, Watson suggests that we should view certain works as failures in order to demonstrate that some of Coltrane's works were problematic and led many musicians up a blind alley. Overall, Watson's aim is to encourage audiences to engage with Coltrane's music with fresh ears; by developing a sense of Coltrane's successes and failings, his mortality is laid bare and we can begin to appreciate the music again.

The need to stress Coltrane's human nature is also expressed by Coltrane's cousin Mary Alexander at the end of Ashley Kahn's book on *A Love Supreme*. Alexander senses an awe-inspired conversation and stresses the fact that Coltrane was "just a man," as if to counter the deification of the artist among cultish fans and obsessive musicians. Although Watson's words were penned in 1991 and Alexander's words were used in Kahn's book in 2002, the Coltrane legacy has continued to go from strength to strength, to the point where the sanctity of Coltrane's life and works remains all-encompassing. As honorable as Watson's desires are for critiquing Coltrane discourse, there is an underlying sense with positions such as these that the overblown rhetoric, piety, and mystification is something divorced from the "music itself." In effect, these types of positions stress that if we can find a way of getting back to the music, the Coltrane legacy will somehow be free from myth-making and hagiographic interpretation. I argue, however, that we cannot simply detach music from its broad social contexts. Rather than seeking to challenge the deification of Coltrane, I suggest that it is per-haps more useful to examine why musicians and audiences feel the need to treat the artist as divine and perpetuate mythologies in this way. Understanding why we need icons or invest jazz with spiritual meaning lies at the core of the Coltrane legacy.

Leonard, for example, tackles this question and discusses the growing secularization of society and urbanization as contributing factors to jazz's growing religiosity. He also discusses the feelings of uncertainty caused by mass migration (for example, of southern blacks to the urban-ized north), the conservative attitudes of the Reagan era, and the gen-eral decline in religious movements. Today, I would argue that the growing power and dominance of the jazz canon, the music's distancing from popular culture, and a reaction to the cult of the media celebrity are additional ways of accounting for the enduring legacy of Coltrane. Coltrane is more important to the jazz tradition today than he has ever been. And yet, his mythologized and simplified representation prevents a critical and in-depth engagement with the artist's life and works. I offer a challenge to this way of viewing Coltrane's work in the next chapter.

CHAPTER 3

Critical Listening

Reviewing the Late Coltrane Recordings

Ironically, while Mingus was outspoken in his militancy, it was Coltrane who became the cultural saint of the late-sixties Black Arts movement, his ascension facilitated partly by his untimely death but even more by the shape of his career. Coltrane's music seemed to move forward in stages toward self-discovery and, for many, toward a fuller awakening of black consciousness.[1]

When in March **1965**, Coltrane appeared at a concert under the rubric "New Black Music," he seemed to validate the most daring music of the time.[2]

With John Coltrane metallic and passionless nullity gave way to exercises in gigantic absurdity, great boring excursions on not-especially-attractive themes during which all possible changes were rung, extended investigations of oriental tedium, long-winded and portentous demonstrations of religiosity....After Coltrane, of course, all was chaos, hatred and absurdity.[3]

John Coltrane's recordings post–*A Love Supreme* occupy an interesting place within his output. On the one hand, the majority of recordings post-1965 signify a departure for Coltrane into "transcendent" territory, both in terms of album concepts and Coltrane's own approach to the creative process. *A Love Supreme* has come to represent the crowning achievement of the Classic Quartet, and subsequent recordings have charted both the expansion and disintegration of the group. Despite the surrounding sadness and regret felt among fans and musicians at the breakup of the Classic Quartet, this late period of Coltrane's life represented a transformation for many followers both in terms of their perception of Coltrane and their own experience of his music. Indeed, the late recordings not only offered a way in to experiencing music on a different level of consciousness but the music also fed directly into the political hotbed of the 1960s, speaking to a generation of race conscious artists and activists who drew on Coltrane's music for inspiration and direct action.

On the other hand, recordings post–A Love Supreme have presented a challenge to musicologists, audiences, and musicians from the moment of their inception to the present day. Not only, rather inevitably, does Coltrane's output take on a different character following the production of A Love Supreme—the music is at times elusive, contradictory, and in opposition to traditional modes of understanding jazz practice—but it is also a body of work that creates problems for historiographers, especially given the predominance of the jazz canon. Regardless of whether A Love Supreme was experienced as Coltrane's magnum opus at the time of its release, the album has gained in symbolic value since the mid-1960s and now marks the end of a creative period, the pinnacle of the achievements of Coltrane and the Classic Quartet. Coltrane's own narrative and surrounding writings on the album portray A Love Supreme as the culmination of his journey since his spiritual awakening in 1957, and other writers have discussed the way in which the album seems to summarize all of Coltrane's musical developments up until that point in a single work. The inclusion of Archie Shepp and Art Davis on the second A Love Supreme recording date also signaled the pathway that Coltrane was to follow, clearly intending to expand the parameters of the group, developing new ways of creating music outside traditional forms, and encouraging collaboration with young and emerging voices. Even though the Classic Quartet would remain together until the end of 1965, the period following A Love Supreme is now represented as a watershed; what was to follow would either be a postlude to what had happened before or a departure into radically new territory.

Recordings post–A Love Supreme have received a range of conflicting responses, from ecstatic and transcendent outpourings to fierce criticism. Although Coltrane received his fair share of negative commentary throughout his career for the development of his musical innovations, his work following A Love Supreme has certainly become associated with a pushing of the creative envelope to beyond the point that many listeners and musicians (including members of the Classic Quartet) could handle. In particular, Coltrane's move toward further experimentation and the embracing of the New Thing has presented a challenge to writers and critics who, since the mid-1960s, have continually searched for an adequate means of interpreting and discussing these recordings both musically and socially. This difficulty has led to Coltrane's later music being cast as abstract and remote. Where, as a canonical work, *A Love Supreme* has clearly been set free of historical time—it is presented as autonomous and timeless—the later recordings are problematic in that, paradoxically, they remain firmly rooted in the social context of the mid- to late 1960s yet can also be understood as transcendent and somewhat abstracted.

To demonstrate the way in which the later recordings have been separated from Coltrane's work up to *A Love Supreme*, one needs only to look at Coltrane's work in the context of jazz education. For example, David Ake has discussed the way in which the establishment of a jazz canon has reified musical standards to the point where abstract and avant-garde forms of jazz are displaced, downplayed, or ignored. In his book *Jazz Cultures*, Ake critically engages with the jazz education system in the United States, where the dominance of chord-scale theory and classically oriented training methods have tended to dominate, in order to illustrate how certain types of knowledge are valued over others.[4] The pursuit of supposedly objective standards for judging jazz performance leads to educators and students focusing mainly on bop and postbop forms as a measure of greatness. Coltrane's *Giant Steps*, for example, has become the benchmark by which musicians judge themselves technically, as the study of chord changes and postbop harmony enables musicians to be (seemingly) evaluated consistently at the technical level, and this technical focus has served to further detach the music from the context of its creation. Ake argues that "jazz pedagogy's classical biases result not only in an incomplete view of John Coltrane's contributions as a musician but, more important, in a narrower understanding of what counts as 'jazz' in America today."[5] By employing a selective view of jazz history in this way, Coltrane's music is misrepresented and we fail to gain an understanding of why works post–*A Love Supreme* have been regarded as the most transcendent and spiritually inspiring for some musicians and listeners.

In a broader historical context, Coltrane's place within the emerging jazz canon was certainly subject to contestation that moved beyond the evaluation of his late recordings. Consider, for example, the following passages from Martin Williams's influential book *The Jazz Tradition*:

> The changes in his work may, of course, have been signs of growth and, if they were, few important jazz improvisers have grown and developed as much as Coltrane did in so short a time. But, on the other hand, the changes may have been naive. Or they may have been signs of personal indecision or frustration.... Perhaps, if his music does not quite reach me and satisfy me as it has

reached some others, the answer is that the gods he sought to invoke are not my gods.[6]

Williams's writings played a significant part in constructing a sense of linear tradition and a canonical framework for jazz.[7] Coupled with this, his role in the creation of the *Smithsonian Collection of Classic Jazz* placed jazz recordings at the heart of historical discourse and provided evidence of the aesthetic and historical value of the music and its seemingly natural progression through time. Somewhat surprisingly, the Smithsonian collection includes only one recording of Coltrane as bandleader ("Alabama") whereas contemporaries such Ornette Coleman have several recordings featured in the collection. The lack of recognition of Coltrane's recorded work, including and beyond *A Love Supreme*, is perhaps tied into Williams's skepticism about Coltrane's contribution to the broader jazz tradition. Indeed, there is an underlying suspicion in Williams's work that Coltrane's quest is too subjective, bordering on the narcissistic. Although describing Coltrane's *Ascension* as the artist's most daring work, Williams openly acknowledged that he admired the deliberately conservative Coltrane who produced the *Ballads* album and collaborated with Duke Ellington.[8] In Williams's view, the jury remained out about Coltrane's embracing of the New Thing.

In contrast to Williams's lukewarm approach to Coltrane's late music, the writings of Amiri Baraka certainly played a significant part in championing the artist's music post–*A Love Supreme*. Baraka was an integral figure in the Black Arts Movement, and his work served to create synergies between artists, poets, and musicians, situating black music at the center of cultural and political life. As a writer, Baraka was a strong advocate of the New Thing, and his writings on black music and musicians such as Coltrane, Archie Shepp, and Albert Ayler were incredibly influential in raising awareness of the politics of race and social class in music and, indeed, American culture at large. Baraka's writings on musicians were powerful in championing an essential blackness that ran through African American music, and his critique of both the white establishment and the social aspiration of the black middle classes changed the grounds upon which jazz was discussed and evaluated.

For Baraka, the blues impulse embodied an abstract form of racial character found in the sense of collective meaning, emotion, and expression of black people. In his influential publications of the 1960s, ranging from his books *Blues People* to *Black Music* (which included his article "The Changing Same [R&B and New Black Music]"), Baraka criticized the "whitening" of the black middle classes who championed the jazz mainstream and promoted a class-oriented race consciousness that grouped the work of R & B artists such as James Brown together with musicians working in the context of New Black Music. Baraka described the way in which black artists were rejecting music that was born out of preexisting attitudes, values, and conventions. In his influential and provocative article "Jazz and the White Critic," Baraka drew attention to the ownership of jazz and attacked a jazz industry that was governed by the white middle classes. Baraka's rebuttal of the status quo included a discussion of the broader contexts within which jazz operated as well as an assertion that there was an essential character to African American experience that could not be understood by white writers. For example, here is Baraka on Coltrane: "The catalysts and necessity of Coltrane's music must be understood as they exist even before they are expressed as music."[9] By arguing that jazz was the result of an attitude or stance within the African American community, Baraka promoted black music as something essential, born out of preexisting values and shared experience. As Lorenzo Thomas has noted, music in this context was presented as the sound of a performed community that enabled writers such as Baraka to view jazz as part of a continuum, linking the music to an ancient African past.[10] Here, it seems entirely natural to discuss Coltrane as a type of griot or to compare jazz performance to African ring shouts; these perspectives promote innate qualities that interpret African American culture as unified, a "changing same."

Despite Williams's skepticism (and, indeed, Baraka's polemics), Coltrane's recordings have become some of the most revered in the continuum of jazz history. As the canon has emerged and the neo-traditionalist agenda has taken a firm grip on the representation of jazz today, Coltrane is presented as the most spiritual of jazzmen. However, even though Coltrane is now arguably perceived as the most iconic of jazz masters, his creative output is still only celebrated in limited terms, evidenced by the way in which only a selection of Coltrane's music finds its way into modern repertoire. Further, the late recordings are practically ignored by musicians today who seek to emulate the work of the past. Eric Nisenson, for example, describes the way in which neo-traditionalists have focused on *A Love Supreme* as the pinnacle of Coltrane's achievements:

> The most dominant, or at least the most famous, jazz musician of our own time, Wynton Marsalis, proclaimed that Coltrane's "free" work of the last couple of years of his life was "Nothin.'" At a recent concert co-produced by Marsalis

devoted to Coltrane's work, all his accomplishments after 1964 were ignored, as if Trane had died after recording *A Love Supreme*.[11]

Ben Ratliff also explains this change in status by suggesting that the late Coltrane recordings are not necessarily perceived as "works" in the way that recordings up until *A Love Supreme* are understood. Like Nisenson, Ratliff draws on the workings of Lincoln Center to illustrate his point: "Lincoln Center is an institution dedicated by definition to repertory, and late Coltrane isn't about repertory, isn't about compositions; it is about sound."[12] Ratliff's observation draws attention to a need for a different aesthetic approach to understanding the late-Coltrane recordings, something I will revisit later on.

More broadly, I would argue that Coltrane's post–*A Love Supreme* recordings are conspicuously absent from the modern jazz tributes, documentary series, and general writings on the qualities and value of the jazz tradition. From the neo-traditionalist perspective, the rejection of Coltrane's work post–*A Love Supreme* has been expressed most strongly in the writings of Stanley Crouch. This is from Stanley Crouch's *Considering Genius*:

> What could have led one of the intellectual giants of jazz...into an arena so emotionally narrow and so far removed from his roots and his accomplishments? While *Interstellar Space*, the 1967 duets session with Ali, are models of their kind,...the other post-mid-1965 recordings, whether studio or live, are largely one-dimensional and do not vaguely compare to what Coltrane accomplished with his Classic Quartet.[13]

The works Crouch refers to in this statement are broad-ranging and varied. All of Coltrane's output from mid-1965 onward is tarred with the same brush, except for Coltrane's duet with Rashied Ali. In this context, Crouch portrays the late period of Coltrane as a type of betrayal and questions the motives of the artist around this time. From a neo-traditionalist perspective, the dissolution of the Classic Quartet and Coltrane's move toward the New Thing are regarded as a rejection of the blues aesthetic of repetition and revision and, as such, the lifeblood of African American experience that has been posited by writers such as Albert Murray and Ralph Ellison.[14] By turning his back on the blues aesthetic and embracing the avant-garde, Coltrane is effectively perceived as taking jazz into a creative cul-de-sac. Within the context of the broader jazz mainstream today, the canonical values promoted by neo-traditionalists clearly affect the way in which recordings are evaluated and understood. Even though musical canons present themselves as naturally occurring and value free, Coltrane's works post–*A Love Supreme* clearly demonstrate how music that does not fit neatly into the ideological framework of the jazz canon are ignored, downplayed, or misrepresented: in many respects, the late recordings serve to highlight the way in which the canon is socially constructed to support particular belief systems.

In contrast to this, I argue that the late works of Coltrane can play a central role in understanding jazz as a discursive cultural practice and in developing an understanding of the ideologies that lie beneath the celebration of jazz as a linear tradition. To demonstrate the way in which Coltrane's recordings post–*A Love Supreme* do not fit easily within the mainstream representation of jazz practice, I draw on examples from three different recording projects and contexts from Coltrane's work from 1965 onward: *Ascension, Interstellar Space,* and *The Olatunji Concert: The Last Live Recording.*

ASCENSION

Coltrane was allowing an informality and spiritualism into his recordings and performances that some found amateurish; others found it freeing and revolutionary.[15]

In many respects, John Coltrane's *Ascension* presents a continuation of the compositional approach and extramusical themes found in *A Love Supreme*. Recorded six months after Coltrane's seminal album on June 28, 1965, *Ascension* is similar to *A Love Supreme* in that it was conceived as an extended "concept album" that moved beyond traditional song forms. *Ascension*, like *A Love Supreme*, also had a pan-religious or spiritually inspired title and theme, and the recording signaled an expansion of the Classic Quartet, this time featuring an 11-musician lineup. Perhaps most strikingly, the opening motivic figure of *Ascension* sounds like a continuation or variation of the *A Love Supreme* theme, providing a sense of musical continuity between the recording projects. Despite the obvious relationship between the two albums, *Ascension* is regarded as seminal for different reasons as, symbolically, the recording marks Coltrane's full embrace of the New Thing and avant-garde playing. As a work, *Ascension* is structured compositionally around a series of chords and related modal scale patterns. As Lewis Porter suggests, changes to modal area are most probably signaled by Coltrane and, although each musician has a solo section within the piece, the ensemble comes together at strategic points within the performance to punctuate solos, signify transitions, and present a collective sound that is fresh, nonhierarchical and rich in texture. As a large-scale work—the two complete takes are each in the region of 40 minutes in duration—*Ascension* was immediately compared to Ornette Coleman's *Free Jazz* due to its extended through-form presentation, enlarged ensemble size, and the promotion of collective or free-form improvisation. Indeed, the comparison to Coleman's work is even cited in A. B. Spellman's liner notes to the album. And yet, as Archie Shepp states in the same note, *Ascension* represents a different conception of ensemble playing that makes the recording unique:

> *Free Jazz* created a new form, and *Ascension* is a further step in the development of that form. John is approaching a group concept of playing—you'll notice that he took no more solo time than anybody else. That's because he didn't want any stars on this record, he wanted a group effect.[16]

Shepp points to the way in which *Ascension* draws out a sense of collectivity that is not present on Coleman's *Free Jazz*. The influential musicologist Ekkehard Jost builds on this idea in his analysis of the differences between *Ascension* and Coleman's *Free Jazz*:

> In the collective improvisations of *Free Jazz*, the contributions of each and every improviser have a certain melodic life of their own; motivic connections and dove-tailing of the various parts create a polyphonic web of interactions. In *Ascension*, on the other hand, the parts contribute above all to the formation of changing sound-structures, in which the individual usually has only a secondary importance.[17]

Despite the monumental nature of *Ascension* and its contextual setting, the recording has been received as problematic or presented with caveats since its release, both through the critical reception of the album and subsequent historical writings. Although most critics at the time recognized the scale, ambition, and significance of *Ascension* in relation to the Classic Quartet's output, there remained a sense of unease about Coltrane's further departure into the experimental sound worlds—and associated politics—of the New Thing. Considering this unease among critics and, indeed, *Ascension*'s many parallels to *A Love Supreme*, it is important to explore the reasons why the album has not come to fulfill a similar role to Coltrane's magnum opus. Moreover, as the reified notion of a jazz canon and tradition has continued to develop from this time, I would argue that the qualified response to *Ascension* can be used as a means of understanding several values that underpin the jazz mainstream today. I suggest that *Ascension* challenges established modes of understanding jazz in the following ways:

1. Questioning Musical Conventions

The most commonly expressed reservation about Coltrane's later recordings is the music's free and unrelenting nature; Coltrane's music challenges established musical conventions to the point where definitions of jazz become fluid and contestable. Coltrane's expansion of the parameters of what was understood as appropriate in a jazz context—presenting extended solos of up to one hour's duration, moving away from established forms and structures, developing polyrhythmic concepts, and so on—was difficult for some fans and commentators to take. Furthermore, when compared to his contemporaries, Coltrane's departure into avant-gardism perhaps signified more of a betrayal to defenders of the tradition; unlike Ornette Coleman or some of the emerging voices that came to embody the New Thing, Coltrane had a proven pedigree: he had "paid his dues" in terms of working as a sideman and ascending through the ranks to become one of the premier postbop artists. Coltrane's subsequent embracing of the experimental nature of the avant-garde represented a challenge to the comfortable jazz narrative where artists develop in a straightforward and linear fashion, each master musician contributing and extending the vocabulary and repertoire of music but remaining firmly within the bounds of the tradition. Against these expectations, *Ascension* challenged established musical conventions by heralding a fascination with sound, bringing other musical parameters such as timbre and texture to the fore.

The experimentation with sound extends beyond the music performed in the studio, and the quest for a unique sound has been described by several writers as an essential ingredient in African American musical circles.[18] Throughout the 1960s, Coltrane demonstrated a meticulous attention to detail in the realization of his sound both inside and outside the studio. Numerous accounts of Coltrane's obsessive practice regimes, from selections of reeds and mouthpieces to scale patterns and choice of fingerings, can understandably be mirrored in his studio work, from the selection of engineers to the choice of takes to the organization of musicians. Several mid-1960s developments signaled a change in attitude toward sound production, and what could be considered new outlets for music in both live and recorded settings, witnessed in the creation of different types of collective including the Black Arts Movement, the AACM, and the Jazz Composers Guild. Moreover, Coltrane's experiments of this time should also be related to the broader artistic and experimental contexts, ranging from Steve Reich's tape experiments to the impact of the British invasion on the US recording industry, from the artist-centered experiments of the Fluxus movement to Glenn Gould's theories about "the prospects of recording." This period offers numerous ways of reframing performance and experimenting with collective practices, questioning the boundaries of what could be considered art.[19]

Despite its monumental nature and the challenging of established conventions, general evaluations of *Ascension* stress that the album has a symbolic importance rather than being a success musically. As Ben Ratliff states, "*Ascension* is not a success in particular. It is hard to get around the tremulous chaos of the group sound, not to mention the many moments of a band whose members are not in sync with one another, reaching points where they might as well stop, but don't. Instead, it is a success in general, a paradigm."[20] The failure to establish the musical credentials of *Ascension* was arguably exacerbated by the confusion over which of the two complete takes to release on the original album. Bob Thiele's selected version was later recalled and replaced by Coltrane's favored choice. Although this provides an interesting insight into the postproduction process, the failure to choose between different takes undermines the value of what Coltrane was doing to level musical parameters. When the music becomes detached from established methods of evaluation, it is difficult to envisage alternative ways of asserting value; we are left with the impression that any take will do. *Ascension* is not about musical detail but collective effect; it provides the listener with a way in to the experimental context of the time and the experiments with sound that were governing Coltrane's studio practices. *Ascension*'s failure to meet the supposedly objective standards of the established canon led to the recording being relegated to a particular historical and social context. Like Schoenberg's venture into atonality in classical music at the beginning of the 20th century, a narrative emerges in which there is a certain inevitability about the album and its place within Coltrane's output; even though it is not regarded as a success musically, "it had to happen" in order for Coltrane to enter the final and tragic stage his career.[21]

2. Challenging Established Hierarchies

On the liner notes to *Ascension*, Archie Shepp suggested that the unique feature of the album is its nonhierarchical nature. Despite Coltrane's reputation as a jazz leader and composer, his participation on the *Ascension* session is sensitive and unassuming. Indeed, Coltrane's involvement in the creation of an ensemble sound is somewhat anti-thetical to the album's cover design, which shows the artist seated alone in quiet contemplation. Like *A Love Supreme*, the cover (though not the spine) is also shot in black and white, the only splash of color reserved for the album's title. The multicolored text provides the only indication of the range of sounds featured on the album.

The collectivity of ensemble playing featured on *Ascension* does not provide any musician with more time than others. Each player has a designated solo spot and the ensemble punctuates each solo section with a collective sounding. Although this type of nonhierarchical experiment is typical of several collective practices in the 1960s, the role that Coltrane fulfils within the sound world of *Ascension* is diamet-rically opposed to canonical aesthetics, where the iconic genius is pre-sented as the center of creativity and performance practice. Ratliff describes the context of the time and offers an explanation for Coltrane's shift in musical approach:

> Jazz had never been less hierarchical. The spirit of musicians' collectives was making obsolete the old story of band-versus-band competition. . . . If there is any truth to the rumors that Coltrane was taking acid between '64 and '67, it would only amount to more similar evidence. LSD commonly encourages the user to see the ideal of life as cooperative and non-hierarchical.[22]

As discussed in chapter 1, Coltrane's drug use presents a number of problems for writers who are interested in presenting history as straight-forward and uncomplicated. Although Lewis Porter refutes the over-blown statement by Miles Davis that "Coltrane died from taking too much LSD," he does suggest that, even though Coltrane's playing remained coherent throughout his later recordings, drug taking might have affected his judgment and attitudinal shifts around this time.[23]

Coltrane's unassuming role within the dynamics of the wider collective proves problematic for canon builders who seek to assert the qualities of experience, reputation, and maturity above youth. Coltrane's nonhierarchical role would not necessarily have been viewed as prob-lematic had his fellow musicians been of equal stature. The remarkable quality of *Ascension*, featuring emerging voices of the New Thing such as Marion Brown, John Tchicai, Archie Shepp, and Dewey Johnson, is also a bone of contention: artists would usually have had to have "paid their dues" in order to share the stage with a musician of the stature of Coltrane. The question of credentials and the eligibility of musicians to perform with Coltrane becomes an integral subtext to his work post–*A Love Supreme* and a significant way of challenging existing hierarchies in jazz. Coltrane's willingness to allow inexperienced musicians to perform with him around this time demonstrates the artist's view that every musician had something valuable to contribute to music. As Spellman states in the liner notes to *Ascension*, "Another thing which John Coltrane has accomplished with *Ascension* is the introduction of several of the most vital of the new voices in jazz. Some of these musicians have recorded, some not. Most are, at this time, unknown outside downtown New York, but *Ascension* should help to rectify that."[24] Drawing on up-and-coming artists who represented the sounds of the New Thing, *Ascension* expressed a different kind of quality, the desire for a sound which summed up many other collective practices of the time.

And yet, the nature of collective improvisation not only caused problems in terms of musical language and a departure into more avant-garde forms, but the authority of the musicians was also brought into question. As Charles Tolliver states, "I felt an intrusion, at first. But it didn't dawn on me until later on that this great man was allowing babies—like, toddlers, crawling—to come onto his stage without feeling any problem about that at all. A lot of us were like, *why*?"[25] Although it could be considered a noble venture to enable contributions by musicians of different standards and backgrounds, the opening up of jazz to different, more inexperienced voices certainly explains the way in which writers such as Stanley Crouch have questioned Coltrane's judgment around this time. There is also a degree of antagonism leveled at the young musicians associated with Coltrane, not only questioning the validity of their contribution but also their right to perform alongside an iconic figure such as Coltrane. David G. Such comments on this criticism in his study of musicians who perform "out there":

> In the 1960s, some musicians were also critical of inexperienced newcomers who were given opportunities to record with major out performers. For instance, hard bop performers castigated Dewey Johnson and Frank Wright when John Coltrane asked them to record with his group in 1965. Rather than first establishing a reputation among hard bop performers as proficient exponents of the hard bop style, Johnson chose instead to explore out approaches to

playing the trumpet. When Coltrane hired him, many hard bop musicians questioned Johnson's lack of experience, unproven technical abilities, and the right to accept Coltrane's offer.[26]

The negative perspectives from established musicians are typified in the words of Philly Joe Jones who argues that, while Coltrane was a specialist who was able to play free music with integrity, the new generation of musicians did not have a command of their instrument:

> I don't think you can play freedom music unless you know your instrument. That was just a door opener. John Coltrane opened the door for a whole bunch of…I call them bag carriers. The bags they carry their instruments in. They've been carrying their horn around for maybe a year. Soon as they get an opportunity, if somebody will allow them to get on a bandstand, they jump on and don't know anything about the horn and just make a bunch of noises.[27]

The negativity leveled at the young musicians associated with Coltrane also ties in with the breakup of the Classic Quartet, with commentators suggesting that artists associated with the New Thing were somehow responsible for the demise of Coltrane's super group. Elvin Jones's often quoted reaction to the *Ascension* session was as a painful experience, and McCoy Tyner's reason for leaving the quartet was that he couldn't hear himself amid a cacophony of sound. Both demonstrate the way in which the direction of Coltrane's music and that of his new associates was becoming antithetical to his established group. Similarly, as Lewis Porter argues, Rashied Ali received a lot of criticism for the breakup of the quartet even though comments leveled at the young drummer were mainly unfounded.[28]

The antagonism toward Coltrane's inexperienced sidemen and the nature of his recordings post *A Love Supreme* extended well beyond Coltrane's lifetime. The writer Francis Davis suggests that, come the 1990s, the majority position on the post-1965 Coltrane was one of confusion and dismay at both the dissolution of the Classic Quartet and their subsequent replacements. To illustrate the mood, Davis draws on a quote from Doug Ramsey: "He was often surrounded by sidemen who were not qualified to be in his company. His music had virtually become pure energy. For the most part, it was impenetrable."[29] The criticism leveled at inexperienced musicians and the general non-hierarchical and inaccessible nature of the music post–*A Love Supreme* clearly stems from the perspective of canonical norms in which virtuosity, experience, musical pedigrees, and a few apprentices (who are privileged enough to get an opportunity to play with jazz masters) have currency.

Coltrane's attitude from mid-1965 onward seems to reject these values, and the music appears to function as something else. These recordings are not about affirming musical genius or the musical credentials of the group. The music is not born out of grand gesture and the celebration of an original work or the singular conception of one great man.[30] Instead, the recordings are discursive; they invite discussion and commentary, and do not fit easily into simple categories. Paradoxically, it is the embracing of the collective spirit and disinterest in affirming canonical values that provides *Ascension* and other late recordings their power: the music foregrounds collectivity and sound. This approach to music making echoes Christopher Small's writings on musicking: by treating music as a verb, the idea of musical "works" existing outside of performed experience becomes redundant. Musicking defies reification and presents musical meaning as integrally linked to the interactions and experiences of musicians, audiences, and the contextual settings where music takes place.[31]

Finally, although Coltrane's strategy of working with inexperienced musicians was criticized at the time and in the years following his death, artists who were bound up with the New Thing—from Archie Shepp to Pharoah Sanders—have subsequently enjoyed successful and critically acclaimed careers in their own right. On the one hand, this clearly demonstrated Coltrane's ability as a talent spotter who nurtured the talents of young artists much in the same way as Art Blakey. On the other hand, I would argue that, unlike Blakey's apprentices, the power of the Coltrane legacy has governed the career trajectories of musicians who played alongside him. Coltrane's overwhelming and unavoidable presence has inevitably shaped the themes of a large number of his apprentices' performance and recording projects.

3. Spirituality, Social and Political Contexts

Although *Ascension* can be seen as mirroring *A Love Supreme* in its spiritual themes and conceptual organization, the challenging of musical convention and overt statements of collective practice served to promote a different form of spirituality that was more closely aligned with the politics and social context of the mid-1960s. In his book *Mercy, Mercy Me*, James Hall describes the way in which, unlike *Ascension*, the themes of love and spirituality in *A Love Supreme* are treated as detached from the social and political context of the time. Although it can be argued that the embracing of religion can be viewed as a form of political statement in its own right, adhering to a different mode of existence that is beyond the influence of dominant American culture and politics, Hall suggests that the accessibility and widespread appeal of *A Love Supreme* resulted in any potential political or social subtext being lost. He states, "The expansiveness of Coltrane's 'love ethic' is potentially swallowed up by the tendency of consumer culture to sentimentalize love or to seek to define it only in terms of the popular romance."[32] *A Love Supreme*'s ability to appeal to different groups results in the album being presented as an offering of universal love. Hall argues that the use of the concept of love as a source of power and direct action, as expressed in the speeches of religious leaders such as Martin Luther King Jr., is lost within readings of *A Love Supreme* and, instead, interpretations of the album are limited to sentimental readings.

With this in mind, *A Love Supreme* can be understood as a work that does not resonate with the social and political sentiment of the times. From 1965, race politics became all the more prevalent in the United States, particularly in cities such as New York. The Student Nonviolent Coordinating Committee (SNCC) leadership moved from being integrationist in nature to more nationalist and confrontational, and writers such as Amiri Baraka moved to Harlem to pursue a more aggressive form of political activism and writing. Placed in its broader context, at a time when the war in Vietnam was beginning to escalate, *A Love Supreme* offered a message that was bound up with a spirit of universalism. Hall continues: "So while critics and celebrants have largely endorsed *A Love Supreme*'s spirituality without question, there is that sense that the recording and composition is just slightly behind the social relevance curve."[33] I would argue that *A Love Supreme*'s detachment enabled the album to be freed from its social context and to be perceived as promoting enduring values of love and universal spirituality.

The works post–*A Love Supreme*, on the other hand, became much more explicitly tied to the social and political context of the time. In his outstanding book *Blowin' Hot and Cool*, John Gennari discusses the context within which albums such as *Ascension* were created and points to the underlying racial anxieties and crises of identity that were felt by many jazz critics of the 1960s. Gennari offers an in-depth analysis of the reception of artists bound up with the New Thing and describes the way in which influential writers and canon builders of the time, such as Whitney Balliett, Dan Morgenstern, and Martin Williams, offered either skeptical or qualified judgments about this new generation of experimental artists. Gennari explains Williams's ambivalence to the music of Coltrane at this time:

> He recognized the bracing effect Coltrane had on his listeners—calling *Ascension* "at the same time a contemporary jazz performance and a communal rite"—but was uneasy about the changes in Coltrane's music that brought him this new impassioned audience, speculating that these changes "may have been signs of personal indecision or frustration."[34]

Gennari comments on the implicit anxiety that several white critics felt at the clear political ramifications of such music.

Whether intended as an overt political statement or not, recordings such as *Ascension* and Coltrane's performances around this time clearly signaled a change in attitude and approach that resonated with the race politics and social turmoil of the mid-1960s. His performance at a benefit concert for the Black Arts Repertory Theater and School in March 1965 provided an explicit endorsement of the movement and the underlying politics at play, and his continued involvement with musicians and artists bound up with avant-gardism and the New Thing signaled an active interest in race politics, if only by association. Lorenzo Thomas demonstrates how musicians such as Coltrane played an integral role in influencing and instigating the militant attitudes of members of the Black Arts Movement. Whether intended or not, the sounds of the New Thing resonated with an entire generation of African American writers, poets, and intellectuals. By lending his name to Black Arts Movement events and initiatives, and championing the work of emerging artists such as Archie Shepp and Marion Brown, Coltrane and his music became inseparable from the political issues of the period. Thomas discusses the way in which Coltrane was exploring possibilities of creating a cooperative booking agency and record label, signifying a desire to reclaim the music on behalf of the musicians who created it.

As canonizers of jazz who had invested a lot of time in promoting the universal qualities of the music, writers such as Williams were reluctant to discuss the social and political dimension of music at this time, choosing to promote the ideal that music both "speaks for itself" and transcends the politics of the everyday world. Within this context, works such as *Ascension* could not help but convey political overtones, both by the way in which the music sounded in comparison to what had occurred before, and by the reception of the music by the musicians who participated in the recording. For example, the *Ascension* session has been described as a catalyst for McCoy Tyner's departure from the group, and he famously went on record to stress that he could not hear himself during the recording session. Debates have raged, both during Coltrane's lifetime and beyond, about the social dimension of the artist's music and whether his music can be interpreted as an overt political statement. Frank Kofsky's famous interview with Coltrane in 1966 was geared heavily toward the political, with the Marxist writer attempting to encourage Coltrane to go on record in his support for Malcolm X and the civil rights movement, and to comment on the broader injustices of the time. Throughout the interview, Coltrane demonstrated an exemplary form of diplomatic response in which his open-ended answers could be interpreted in several ways.

And yet, despite Coltrane's reluctance to go on record as a political activist, the context within which the music was produced and received *was* overtly political and this was something that critics of the music could not ignore. By aligning himself with a new generation of artists, Coltrane was effectively reinventing himself: the mere championing of the work of race conscious musicians such as Shepp can be understood as an explicitly political act, constituting empathy—at the very least— with the cause. Coltrane's fascination with players of the New Thing— Albert Ayler, Rashied Ali, Archie Shepp—was an indication of his desire to broaden the spectrum of sound creation, and he went on record to express his interest in developing musical compositions that blended the old with the new. The strong degree of political activism and perspective of the musicians Coltrane was associating with certainly cannot be downplayed. Although we might not consider the musicians as speaking from one voice—for example, John Tchicai stressed that his own view of black nationalism was very different from Archie Shepp's—Coltrane obviously would have been aware of politics by association, which in part explains critics' and musicians' reactions to the album.

The spiritual themes presented in *Ascension* become inseparable from the context of the time and signal a more direct form of intervention and engagement. *Ascension* paves the way for other late works in that it anticipates and counters the problems Hall identifies with *A Love Supreme*. The recording is noncompromising, not prone to sentimental interpretations, and therefore not readily adapted into the narratives of canon builders and traditionalists who promote jazz as beyond politics, a music that expresses universal values and can "speak for itself." The release of *Ascension* can also be understood against a wider backdrop of experimentation that was taking place in the mid-1960s, and the collective spirit of the album was evidenced in other activities of the time, ranging from the work of Bill Dixon in establishing collectives such as the Jazz Composers Guild and staging events such as the October Revolution in Jazz, to artists seeking to rewrite the rule book by using traditional forms of media (such as recordings) in new ways or seeking new outlets for their art.[35] Although Coltrane was not formally associated with the Jazz Composers Guild, he was said to have had empathy with the cause and championed the New Thing in different ways. Coltrane performed as part of the October Revolution in Jazz and also used his influence at Impulse records to broker contracts for emerging artists such as Archie Shepp.

INTERSTELLAR SPACE

Interstellar Space was recorded in February 1967 as a series of six duets with the drummer Rashied Ali. The album was released posthumously and was most probably intended to be a suite in the same vein as *A Love Supreme*, this time with the spiritual theme taking on a more cosmological order. *Interstellar Space* is one of the most celebrated of the late recordings and Impulse's posthumous Coltrane releases. As stated earlier, the breakup of the Classic Quartet raised a question mark about Coltrane's direction and the credentials of the musicians he was surrounding himself with toward the end of his life. And yet the six duet recordings with Ali serve as a vindication of Coltrane's choices and direction, in that they clearly demonstrate the full glory of Coltrane's late style. *Interstellar Space* embodies several of the characteristics of the post–Classic Quartet style: the music moves away from set meter and regular beat and there is no clear sense of modality, harmonic change, or tonal center. The instrumentation of saxophone and percussion duet helps to support this new approach, as the combination naturally encourages a different conception of playing that focuses on timbre and texture rather than harmony and melody. The album is a striking contrast to *Ascension*, in that it moves away from the broad-based scale patterns and tonal structures, toward a more abstract approach to sound production. The recording has a seductive quality, particularly in the way in which the energy of the two musicians is channeled and the contrasting dynamics move from a reflective whisper to a sheer invasion of sound space.

Despite the album's clarity of purpose and critical acclaim (as evidenced through Stanley Crouch's endorsement), *Interstellar Space* also presents problems for canon builders and writers who are interested in constructing easily digestible historical narratives. To demonstrate this, I will focus on two aspects of *Interstellar Space* that problematize existing approaches to the study of recorded jazz and the place of Coltrane's late music in jazz history.

1. Recording as Process, Not Product

In his study of the life and music of John Coltrane, Lewis Porter provides a valuable insight into the musical design and architecture of *Interstellar Space*, and describes the album as "the ideal starting place for the listener who wants to understand Coltrane's last music."[36] The clarity of recording is aided by the duet format: when stripped down to two instruments, Coltrane's performance techniques and improvisatory devices are more readily identifiable, and the clarity and intensity of sound remains consistent throughout. Through a detailed analysis of sections of *Interstellar Space*, Porter sheds light on many of the musical devices Coltrane employed at this time, from fast repetitive descending scales to rapid changes in register, and he argues that a lot of Coltrane's material at this point in time is difficult to place into neat analytical categories. However, on repeated listening, I would agree with Porter in his claim that there is continuity in Coltrane's approach to improvisation at this time, and that the artist has not necessarily changed from his pre-*A Love Supreme* recordings.

For example, Coltrane's improvisations often develop from small cell-like patterns that are extended through a range of rhythmic and motivic permutations.[37] However, the removal of identifiable structures, a steady pulse, and clear sense of meter opens up the music and removes familiar aids of orientation for the listener. In this respect, although Coltrane's sound and approach can be understood as part of the same continuum, the context has changed dramatically to the point where the music is clearly experienced more as an immediate sensation. This leads to recordings such as *Interstellar Space* being received as musical processes rather than as products; they encourage us to listen in the here and now as opposed to assimilating what has happened before and predicting what will happen next. Ben Ratliff describes the nature of Coltrane's late work:

> It is not really meant to be recorded—such enormities can't be frozen and sold in measured units—yet the recordings are transcendent in spite of themselves. Resistance or intolerance toward this music is a kind of sclerosis; to open oneself to it is to admit honesty and greater feeling. "Understanding it" is empirical Western foolishness; the will to understand is just more sclerosis.[38]

Experiencing a recording as a type of *music as process* counters the canonical imperative of reifying music; Coltrane's music does not convey a singular meaning or set of values but works as an agent for questioning and opening up the discourse about what music could be. In Coltrane's world at this time, the studio becomes a site for investigation and discovery, and the duets with Ali convey a clear sense of experimentation and interplay between two creative artists. The experimental nature of the recordings on *Interstellar Space* is best summed up by Francis Davis on the liner notes to the 2000 reissue, who states that, for Coltrane, "the studio was every bit as much a workshop as the nightclub bandstand.... But the studio offered him an opportunity for experimentation of a different sort, becoming a place of great value to him as a bandleader and a composer."[39]

Even though Porter's transcriptions of *Interstellar Space* offer impressive musical insights into the structure and thematic development of Coltrane's solos, there is a definite sense that notation alone cannot capture the intensity, energy, and sound encountered when listening to the recording firsthand. Although *Interstellar Space* is an extreme example, the experience of the schism between notation and sonic experience should not be limited to this example. Indeed, by experiencing *Interstellar Space* in this way, we can come to understand the inadequacy of notation in relation to all recorded music: transcription fails to convey the power of jazz on record in all its forms. As a sonic experience, *Interstellar Space* has a rich, sensual quality that clearly explains Coltrane's fascination with sound. More than any other late Coltrane recording, *Interstellar Space* draws the listener in with its sensuous sounds and demonstrates the way in which recordings can open our ears to different listening experiences. The experience of the recording as a type of process is also exacerbated by the posthumous release of the album; a question mark remains over the work's "completeness," and, if Coltrane had intended the album to be a type of planets suite, there is no knowing the size and scale of this project or how the artist would have organized the material as part of an authorized release.

2. Cosmology and Transcendence

Conceptually, Coltrane's late recordings blend themes of spirituality with cosmology. There is a clear move from the overt offerings and devotion to God found on *A Love Supreme* toward a form of transcendent mysticism. Despite the different approaches and makeup of groups, Coltrane recordings released posthumously such as *Sun Ship, Stellar Regions, Cosmic Music, Transition*, and the controversial *Infinity* are all suggestive of a change in perception of the artist's status. The later recordings provide a platform for Coltrane to be represented as "otherworldly," both drawing inspiration from the metaphysical world and embarking on a quest for deeper meaning and understanding in music. Coltrane's perceived transcendent status has played a significant part in the construction of his saintly presence and the posthumous nature of many of the late releases certainly enhances the process of deification.

Despite the hagiographic writings and otherworldly persona, Coltrane's representation as transcendent relates directly to some African American music in the late 1960s and early '70s, where themes of space and cosmology were employed as strategies of resistance and political empowerment. Sun Ra, for example, famously claimed that he was descended from Saturn and used the metaphor of space to convey themes of ancient wisdom, Africa, slavery, and oppression. "Space," therefore, provided a powerful symbol for artists, enabling them to resist existing cultural and political ideas and present black subjects as outside the system. James Hall explains the way in which artists were seeking to step outside existing paradigms:

> Unable to fully enjoy the experience of full selfhood, agency, and citizenship... many African-American creative intellectuals were forced to radically reevaluate their relationship to nation, race, and even mode of living. By the 1960s, this sense of being at the precipice became, for some, a necessary, sweeping antimodernism, a provocative counterstatement.[40]

By drawing on cosmology and themes of spirituality and mysticism, artists such as Ra and Coltrane were not merely expressing an interest in other worlds as generated by the space race but were presented as exploring higher modes of existence. Their leadership, in turn, attracted cultish devotion from fans and musicians alike. Spirituality, or the elegiac mode, can be understood as a response to modernity and dismissal of the past; these themes foreground the possibility of transformation through art and the potential for social change. For Coltrane, space is a powerful symbol that charts his transition from spiritual to transcendent artist.

Although the interest in space can be interpreted as a political strategy—placing oneself outside existing cultural and political paradigms—themes of transcendence and cosmology can be understood as problematic for the historian in several ways. First, by seeking to step outside the politics of the white American mainstream with themes of transcendence and cosmology, the social and political impact of music could be undermined. For example, by repeatedly stressing that he was a "different order of being," Ra could appear disengaged from the social political context of the late '60s and early '70s. In Coltrane's case, Hall has suggested that the new patterns of "space" to emerge in Coltrane's music were part of a reimagining, a development of a new mythology bound up with the artist. Hall's thesis is that the strategies of some African American artists around this time were antimodern, direct rejections of existing cultural paradigms. While acknowledging the decline of album titles rooted in African American culture, Hall also suggests that a possible criticism of late Coltrane could be his perceived distancing or dismissal of uniform or core African American values. This change in perception had the disappointing effect of portraying the music as unlistenable or disconnected from the past.

Second, and following on from the last point, I argue that separating Coltrane's later work from his earlier period creates an unnecessary schism between the transcendent Coltrane and his earlier work. Inevitably, this distancing leads to a devaluing of the later works, especially given the fact that *A Love Supreme* is represented as the artist's crowning achievement. As discussed earlier, the fact that the majority of the space-inspired recordings were released posthumously also leaves a question mark over this output, as the issue of authorial intent remains unresolved. Although the same issues apply to a certain extent within all recorded releases, the mediated nature of the late Coltrane recordings—be it the involvement of Alice Coltrane or the place of Coltrane within the revised marketing strategies of Impulse—is clear for all to see.

Finally, portraying Coltrane's music as transcendent serves not only to distance the music from the sociopolitical context of the 1960s, but also to fuel the problematic fantasies of creativity that lead to black culture being treated as unchanging, mysterious, and beyond discourse. As Ronald Radano states,

> In political terms, the metaphysical claims of black music that became emblematic of the Black Arts Movement challenged a vulnerable white supremacy that could no longer explain away the power and appeal of black musical achievement. As enabling as these racial essentialisms may have been, however, they also constrained the comprehension of black music's more fundamental insurgencies, particularly with reference to the undermining of racial categories.[41]

The influence of space and cosmology on the music of John Coltrane, coupled with an array of cultural influences from Indian music to European classical music to Africa, could easily be seen to challenge established racial categories and well-trodden expectations of black music. Hall reinforces this idea by claiming that the antimodern strategies of many African American artists presented alternatives to established ideas about black history that made "constructions of any essential blackness (and indeed any monolithic construction of African American culture) increasingly difficult to swallow."[42]

With Coltrane's untimely death, however, the opportunity to celebrate different subject positions soon gave way to the perpetuation of essentialist discourse. Indeed, there was a subsequent reification of Coltrane's persona, and his representation was reclaimed and controlled to the point where he is now typically portrayed only in limited terms. According to Scott Saul, "While Coltrane was loath to attach his music to a specific political ideology, preferring a language of universal spirituality, he became posthumously an icon of a uniquely black epistemology."[43] Coltrane was claimed by writers, musicians, and poets alike as the embodiment of pure African American values: from the writings of Baraka through to biographers such as Simpkins, from Coltrane poets to recent scholarly readings of the artist's music, Coltrane is foregrounded as the embodiment of an essential African American spirit.

Despite Hall's identification of a range of black American subject positions and antimodernism's ability to challenge essentialist discourses, the influence of the Black Arts Movement on writings and interpretations of figures such as Coltrane proved significant. The need for a type of political essentialism far outweighed the subtle challenges to racial categories found within African American arts at this time. Coltrane's familial links to the black church and his later incarnation as a questing, transcendent being also offered a powerful vehicle for promoting African American experience as uniform, unaltered by time and existing by its own set of rules. I argue that these essentialisms inhibit Coltrane, his representation and place within broader cultural discourse, and present the artist as detached from the everyday world, only to be appreciated by a select few.[44] In challenging the racial categories of music and established paradigms, Radano continues: "Such thinking brings us dangerously close to arguing that black music is something that lies beyond the cultural mainstream and thus necessarily outside the realm of American experience overall."[45] Today, the challenge is to understand the need for political essentialism as a strategy to combat racism but not to let readings of African American music be limited to essentialist paradigms. By freeing up Coltrane's late music in this way, we can understand how themes of cosmology and transcendence have been used to separate Coltrane from the complexities and contradictions of lived experience and to promote blackness as mysterious, beyond discourse. I will revisit these themes in the final chapter.

THE OLATUNJI CONCERT: THE LAST LIVE RECORDING

The Olatunji Concert presents a range of interesting issues for musicologists and historiographers. As Coltrane's last published recorded project and public performance put on record, the recording presents a snapshot of the artist just months before his death in July 1967. *The Olatunji Concert* recording documents the first part of a two-part concert that was given on April 23, 1967, at the newly opened Olatunji Center of African Culture in New York. The concert served as a fundraiser for the center—which was named after its founder, the musician Babatunde

Figure 3.1:
John Coltrane Sextet last live recording at the Olatunji African Cultural Center in Harlem, NYC, April 23, 1967. Photo courtesy of Rashied Ali, Yasuhiro "Fuji" Fujioka collection.

Olatunji—and involved Coltrane's new quartet of Alice Coltrane, Jimmy Garrison, and Rashied Ali, alongside Pharoah Sanders and Algie Dewitt on bata drum.

As well as feeding into issues raised above concerning collectivity, music as process and references to Africa, the Olatunji Concert recording presents several unique problems.

1. Fidelity and Finality

The idea of a last work acting as a summary or a capstone is a sweet and hopeful construct. But life doesn't add up for the living.[46]

In many respects, *The Olatunji Concert* can prove a frustrating experience for the listener. Only half of the concert was captured on record, and the fidelity of sound is a major cause for concern. As a final offering, the inconsistent, continually changing "live" recording seems like a million miles away from the controlled, engineered, and edited *A Love Supreme*. Contrasting the two recordings provides the listener with an immediate way into understanding the role of mediating forces within different recording contexts. *A Love Supreme* is clean, polished, well-preserved, and complete; the album is consistently engineered, balanced, and edited and presented as a coherent whole. *The Olatunji Concert*, on the other hand, is incomplete and variable in sound quality. The sound of musicians playing live is interspersed with audience noise and sounds of traffic leaking in from outside the venue. Recording engineer Bernard Drayton discussed the way in which he had to switch off one of the stereo channels in order to limit the amount of external noise, and the result is one of continual change in recording conditions. In terms of musical sound, *The Olatunji Concert* presents an imbalance of recording quality that results in the saxophones of Coltrane and Sanders and percussion sounds of Ali and Dewitt overpowering the sounds of the piano. Garrison's bass sound is obscured through distortion, and at various stages it is difficult to distinguish between intended sounds and unintentional noise. Although issues of balance, audience noise, and fidelity are all part of the experience of "liveness" on a live album, with *The Olatunji Concert* recording these factors are foregrounded to the extent that inconsistencies and the incomplete nature of the recording process are on show for all to hear. These frustrations do not sit well with listeners wishing to hear Coltrane's final offering as something pure, unadulterated, and complete. Within this context, it is easy to understand how *A Love Supreme* has taken on the symbolic importance of a last work, as the themes associated with the album and production standards remain clear and tightly focused.

With *The Olatunji Concert*, it is difficult to know what purpose the recording was intended for. Coltrane had employed engineer Bernard Drayton at short notice to record the concert outside of Coltrane's contractual obligations with Impulse records, so the question remains as to whether this recording was to be used for general release or as a simple documentation of a live performance event.[47] The reception of *The Olatunji Concert* is affected by the feeling of listening to a recording that was probably intended for private consumption. Despite the unease caused by the recording quality and the circumstances of its production, the documentation of the concert does carry historical significance, as the event provided Coltrane's only public appearance in New York in 1967 and his penultimate public engagement before his death in July that year. As Coltrane's final documented performance, the recording raises as many questions as it finds answers. Not only was the performance only partially recorded, but there is also a question mark over whether this recording is Coltrane's final recorded statement. Porter's discographical work, for example, shows that Coltrane entered the Van Gelder studio on May 17 and recorded two tracks; the session, along with two other recording sessions in spring of 1967, remains missing or misplaced.[48]

2. Afrocentrism and the Politics of the Popular

The Olatunji Concert also raises questions about Coltrane's influences at the time of his death as well as the relationship between his late style and earlier music. Contrary to my discussion earlier about the dissolution of the essential black subject, Coltrane's presence at a concert in support of the newly opened Olatunji Center of African Culture seems to validate those perspectives that place the artist at the heart of the continuum of black African influence. Coltrane was clearly an advocate for initiatives that would empower black communities and serve to support disenfranchised voices. As mentioned earlier, at this time Afrocentric themes were also used interchangeably with the exploration of cosmology and spirituality: the symbolic use of space and ship metaphors served to convey the passage of slavery and feelings of displacement, and of a subject without a homeland. However, writings that celebrate Coltrane's Afrocentricity tend to create a divide between the artist's pre–*A Love Supreme* works and his later venture into the New Thing. The late style is portrayed as Coltrane's way of destroying his former self, like an act of self-discovery and political reinvention, reinforcing Amiri Baraka's statement that "New Black Music is this: Find the self, then kill it."[49] Baraka's view of Coltrane was of a type of murderer or anarchist, "whose anarchy seems so radical because references to the 'old music' still remain."[50] In other words, when the avant-garde-inspired Coltrane played repertoire linked to his earlier career, the material had been radically transformed to such an extent that he (and his music) had become unrecognizable.[51] The discovery and celebration of Afrocentric themes through extended techniques and avant-garde playing is frequently set up in opposition to Coltrane's more commercial pursuits. African themes, therefore, provide a way of demonstrating an "other" history that is beyond the influence of white commercial, capitalist America.

In his article, "When Bar Walkers Preach: John Coltrane and the Crisis of the Black Intellectual," Tommy Lott feeds off the black avant-garde versus commercialism binary by stating that Coltrane was "transforming an entertainment practice into an intellectual endeavour that conceptually advanced black music.... His transition from a traditional bebop style of playing jazz to a radical avant-garde modernist approach was a necessary step required to accommodate his ongoing reconception of earlier ideas, representing a process of revising his earlier work."[52] Lott argues that Coltrane rejects his earlier self during the latter period as a way of stressing a growing intellectual assertiveness, affirming the sensibilities of his black preacher self and rejecting the entertainment industry.

Coltrane clearly demonstrated an interest in Africa, both in terms of his musical interests and community work; however, interpreting these influences as a form of anticommercialism appears off the mark, especially when listening to the two tracks recorded as part of *The Olatunji Concert*. The first half of the concert featured a performance of Coltrane's "Ogunde" followed by "My Favorite Things." Coltrane's inclusion of "My Favorite Things" could be interpreted as an example of Baraka's destruction of the self, in that performance is clearly delivered as an abstract concept, typical of his latter style. When listening to the recording, however, the performance clearly does not destroy Coltrane's former self or previous incarnations of the popular hit. I would argue that the way in which "My Favorite Things" is treated musically within the concert setting is a clear sign of a connection with the past, rather than fragmentation.

The concert performance begins with an extended bass solo and, once the ensemble begins performing, there are few musical signifiers that would lead the audience to the familiar sound world of the Rodgers and Hammerstein tune or the world of Coltrane's Classic Quartet. And yet, through the extended improvisation and cacophony of sound, the piece offers a dynamism and sense of purpose for over 30 minutes that culminates in a final statement of the "My Favorite Things" tune complete with the same phraseology and musical gesture as found on Coltrane's album for Atlantic. The theme is sounded out at the end of the piece as an act of affirmation, a cathartic moment in an intense and highly charged performance. Within this context, the performance cannot be interpreted as an act of destruction, as "My Favorite Things" appears triumphant at the close of the work. This musical display feeds into broader questions about Coltrane's relationship with his pre–*A Love Supreme* works and the artificial divisions that have been created since the artist's death as well as the futility of seeking a uniform understanding of Coltrane's output. As Ratliff suggests, it is naive to describe the *Olatunji Concert* as honest, or as an act of resistance or inclusion: the picture is more complicated, as any interpretations are ultimately reductive and miss out on the complexity of the moment.[53]

When considering interpretations of Coltrane as embodying an essential blackness and rejecting commercialism, it is important to explore underlying agendas and the foundations on which different perspectives are based. For example, consider the way in which the concept of blackness itself can be seen as a type of commodity, born out of a historical and cultural dialogue that has been shaped by a problematic worldview.[54] When viewed in these terms, contrasting blackness as a type of underlying commodity in opposition to the commercialization of Coltrane's earlier career seems redundant and wide of the mark. Instead, the complexity of Coltrane's interests and a variety of messages come to the fore; the presence of Afrocentric themes, commercial hits, cross-cultural references, cosmology, and mysticism highlight the discursive nature of jazz and the way in which the music means different things to different people at different times.

INTERTEXTUALITY AND THE LATE RECORDINGS

Coltrane's work post–*A Love Supreme* presents a number of challenges for listeners, musicians, and musicologists as the music does not always conform to established expectations about what jazz recordings should be. Moreover, the late recordings also raise fascinating questions about the path Coltrane's music was beginning to take. In many ways, the post–*A Love Supreme* recordings are rich in thematic content and display a sound world full of contrasting sonorities and textures. Musician Dave Liebman discusses Coltrane's mature style:

> By the time of *A Love Supreme* or this [late] period, the vestiges of his roots or of our roots, meaning what we have to do to play, are pretty much hidden. It is not that they are not there, it is just that you don't know them. But they are there, they are just submerged, which of course is one of the great goals of an artist: to take his roots and submerge them into his own language. Only the experts can tell where they are coming from. I don't know anybody else who has been able to do that in the history of this music.[55]

Although the Coltrane sound is something that is clearly distinguishable, I would argue that the suggestion that only experts can tell where Coltrane is coming from contributes only to the feeling that the late music is impenetrable and difficult for mainstream audiences. Rather than viewing Coltrane's roots as submerged—as Liebman describes—I would suggest that that musical influences are multilayered, reconstituted, and recontextualised in the late recordings, as they present listeners with a rich variety of sounds that blend different musical influences.

Indeed, several late recordings either appear to be reworkings of the same musical ideas or present material that directly references Coltrane's previous work. For example, posthumously released recordings such as *Expression* and *Stellar Regions* offer glimpses into a sophisticated sound world where influences merge, concepts of originality are blurred, and listening becomes a sensuous and overtly intertextual experience. The track "Offering," which appears on the recordings *Expression*—the last album sanctioned for release by Coltrane—and *Stellar Regions*, provides a useful example of intertextuality in Coltrane's late style. "Offering" begins with a direct quotation of the opening fanfare motif of *A Love Supreme*, and the material is used as both an explicit reference to the past and as a new point of departure. By taking one fragment of a previous composition and developing a new piece from the material, Coltrane encourages listeners to relate to the past in the present. With the meanings that *A Love Supreme* had accrued, even at this time, the use of the "Acknowledgement" fanfare moves immediately beyond straightforward quotation toward an explicit link to Coltrane's seminal work in both musical and spiritual terms. As an "Offering," the reference to *A Love Supreme* places current listening in relation to other recording experiences and musical influence becomes a two-way phenomenon: the present experience informs the past as much as the past informs the present. This intertextual reference is echoed in different tracks on the *Stellar Regions* album, as several compositions blend *A Love Supreme*–inflected thematic material with free-flowing structures that stem from post-*Ascension* works. For example, the opening track on *Stellar Regions*, "Seraphic Light," opens with a simple repetitive minor pentatonic theme, the use of which can be heard as a stripped down version of both the *A Love Supreme* and *Ascension* themes.

Similarly, the title track "Stellar Regions" also presents material that was to appear on Coltrane's *Interstellar Space*, recorded the week after this session. The "Stellar Regions" theme—which is colored by a slow, accelerating trill on the 5th and 6th degree of a major mode—is also the theme for Coltrane's "Venus" on *Interstellar Space*.

While the reworking of compositional material into different performance contexts is not new to jazz, I argue that these posthumous releases offer glimpses into a musical style in which different musical aesthetics converge. Following the breakup of the Classic Quartet, Coltrane explained his objectives in an interview with Frank Kofsky:

> There was a thing I wanted to do in music, see, and I figured I could do *two* things: I could have a band that played like the way we used to play, and a band that was going in the direction that this, the one I have now is going—I could combine these two, with these, you know, with these two concepts going. And it could have been done.[56]

During the interview, Coltrane expresses a degree of regret of the breakup of the Classic Quartet and suggests that musical synthesis was central to his musical aesthetic at this time. When listening to Coltrane's posthumous releases, I would argue that this vision is realized, as thematic simplicity and reflective beauty seamlessly merge with complex phrases and extended techniques. The contrasts in musical style are not contrived or deliberate but entirely integrated. By referencing earlier materials or playing standards, such as "My Favorite Things" at the *Olatunji Concert*, Coltrane manages simultaneously to draw reference to previous recordings, conjuring up relationships to the past, and, in turn, uses these experiences as a new point of departure. More interesting, the musical vocabulary is not one that rejects the past or critiques previous performances, but the musical style focuses on points of commonality and thematic similarity that can be understood as a type of compositional cosmopolitanism. Here, the structures are "free" and polyrhythmic and the work of Coltrane's ensemble is multilayered, not conforming to traditional accompaniment roles. I would also suggest that Coltrane's late music resists another binary: it is as melodic as it is unmelodic, it looks to the past as it does to the future, and, more important, it offers listeners a glimpse into the infinite combinations and permutations of what music can be.

ALTERNATIVE PASTS, ALTERNATIVE FUTURES: LISTENING AS A DISCURSIVE ACT

When understanding the problems that recordings post–*A Love Supreme* create for historians writing within the jazz canon, I argue that it is important to get away from established modes of thinking in order to develop a different sensibility toward Coltrane's music. Understanding the way in which Coltrane's albums can disrupt and challenge existing paradigms is a useful starting point for thinking about his recordings in a different light. By exploring the complexities and contradictions of the social and political environments in which the albums were created, as well as subsequent mythmaking processes, it is possible to develop new modes of critical listening that both help to situate the recordings in their historical context and also liberate the recordings from the confines of the neo-traditionalist agenda. For example, to establish a sense of discourse and critical listening, it is important to consider how collectivity in music or the mediating factors of the recording process disrupt our experiences and expectations. If we develop an understanding of the ideological function of music and the types of mythologizing and remythologizing that occur over time, we can also develop an awareness of our own mythmaking tendencies and the way in which we project desires and imagined narratives onto our listening experiences.

In seeking alternatives to established modes of listening and understanding, we can use the late Coltrane recordings as a way into reexamining experiences of all recorded jazz, hearing alternative pasts as well as imagining alternative futures for music. In unpacking this idea, consider Nat Hentoff's retrospective view of Coltrane's late work from 1976 and its impact on listeners:

> Coltrane kept looking and finding, and, never satisfied, looked some more. His audience was growing, especially among musicians, but more nonmusicians were finding that if they *actively* listened to his music, their whole way of hearing

jazz might well be changed.... I suggested that those who were finding Coltrane "difficult" start again, but this time without worrying about how it is all structured, where it's leading. Let the music come in without any pre-set definitions of what jazz *has* to be, of what *music* has to be.[57]

Hentoff advocates a form of experimental listening in which audiences approach music without any preconceived notions of what music can be: they need to take the same risks in challenging convention as the musicians on record. Although I admire Hentoff's advice for listeners to throw off the shackles of convention, as listeners we cannot help but be bound, to some extent, by our previous listening experiences.

In taking Hentoff's advice, I would argue that retaining a creative tension between conditioned experience and a resistance to convention offers a way in to understanding listening as a type of discursive practice. I suggest that the late recordings can provide audiences with an alternative mode of listening that can be applied retrospectively to all recorded experiences. The late Coltrane recordings engender a type of discursive listening because they present a challenge to existing musicological practices (such as transcription and analysis) and do not sit comfortably within the canonical model of "great" works that stand alone and which are produced by singular creative geniuses. Listening to late Coltrane recordings, not only do we become aware of the mediating factors that feed into the production of records, but we also become acutely aware of our own subjective position in relation to the music being played. When listening to *The Olatunji Concert*, we become aware of the different subject positions of those involved in the event. For example, the constant physical movement of the microphone and tampering with the stereo channels, the audience noise and street sounds, the imbalance of musical instruments and blurring of intended and nonintended sounds all serve to offer the listener a range of different perspectives on the performance.

Although I would agree with Ratliff, who argues that we should not interpret *The Olatunji Concert* as "honest" because of its raw sense of liveness, I suggest that experiencing different subjectivities enables us to listen discursively, developing a sense of aural perspective and the conflicting and mediating forces at play. Critical listening, therefore, is not just about understanding the social and historical discourse of the music we hear, or making sense of the stories and mythologies that are embedded in different musical experiences, but also an attempt to listen with fresh ears. In adopting a discursive approach to listening, we can hear music in its historical context with renewed vigor, and we can newly appreciate the quality of sound in any given moment. For critical listeners, engaging with jazz on record is not only a discursive act but also an integral part of the musicking of people. In opening our ears to elements of sound, texture, dynamism, as well as the process of mediation, Coltrane's late recordings have the ability to captivate, seduce, and re-energize listening experiences.

And yet they can also encourage us to ask questions both of ourselves, and the music and musicians we identify with. Following the death of Coltrane, several writers and critics have been arguing for a demystification of the artist, encouraging a form of resistance to romanticized and saintly depictions of his life and works. Engaging with late Coltrane discursively, it is possible to develop insights into the seductive nature of these recordings, how they have been promoted and received as transcendent by musicians and fans alike, and how listeners have responded both violently and reverently following exposure to these sounds. In this context, critical listening meaningfully reconnects Coltrane to the complexities and contradictions of everyday life.

CHAPTER 4

A Love Supreme Remixed

"One thought can produce millions of vibrations," wrote Coltrane on *A Love Supreme*. So can a song, a sound, and even a catchy record title. References to and echoes of the album abound forty years after its release. Its elements have been borrowed with enough regularity and variety to warrant its current status as a cultural touchstone. By all indications, Coltrane's count was not far off.[1]

Since Coltrane's death in 1967, *A Love Supreme* has influenced such a large number of people and fed into such a range of artistic and cultural pursuits that, today, the album has become a symbol for a number of related values and beliefs. Within this final chapter, I explore the breadth of this influence and the way in which Coltrane's seminal recording has inspired a generation of people working both inside and beyond the reaches of the jazz community. I argue that the power and widespread impact of *A Love Supreme* demonstrates the way in which recordings can transform cultures, and even our view of history itself, and come to stand for a host of values that lie beyond the experience of music as a sonic encounter. In effect, the power of recorded jazz lies not only in the quality of sound and the music on display but in its interrelationship with broader cultural narratives. As Ronald Radano suggests,

> When we listen to a jazz performance at a club like the Village Vanguard, we hear the music through the lens of history, as the space provides a kind of accompanying sound track to the sound itself. Or, perhaps more accurately, we hear the club in the music, given that we can never really separate our stories of the music from its seemingly pure sonic form.[2]

Developing this idea, we can begin to understand how meanings—values, beliefs, narratives, and so on—are developed from listening to recordings and, subsequently, how those meanings can take on a form of their own over time. More than any other jazz album, *A Love Supreme* has inspired responses of a particular type, its musical themes and associated narratives providing inspiration for works of music, literature, poetry, and film.

The timing of Coltrane's death became a critical factor in the development and representation of Coltrane and his legacy. Indeed, as Bill Shoemaker argued, "Coltrane dying as his music reached such a spiritually fervoured apex makes a neat package out of a complex artistic odyssey."[3] Building on this, the premature death of Coltrane not only led to reappraisals of *A Love Supreme*, an inevitable reordering of the work in relation to Coltrane's full and final career trajectory, but it also sparked a wave of anguish and turmoil among different musical and artistic groups. As a cultural and spiritual icon, Coltrane's death left a void that could not be filled by other musicians or artistic leaders.

Further, the mythic persona of Coltrane had already started to develop during his lifetime as writers such as Amiri Baraka had used the artist as a central figure in the development of an aesthetic for the Black Arts Movement. Come the mid-1970s, writings on Coltrane were filled with overblown and romanticized statements about him. Indeed, "Trane" had become a mythic persona, a godlike figure who was tied integrally to the African American tradition. Bruce Tucker offers the following reading of Coltrane biographies of the mid-1970s:

J. C. Thomas's *Chasin' the Trane* (1975) is typical. Like many books written about charismatic artists, *Chasin' the Trane* all too often leaves its ostensible subject behind in favor of narcissistic effusions from the author and his friends about their feelings regarding the master. The book is an assemblage of narrative and quotations, many of them from people with only the most tenuous connection to Coltrane. It includes not only some pointless and pretentious lyrics to "Blue Train" written long after Coltrane's death, but it treats the reader to Coltrane's horoscope as well. In sum, it is a self-conscious and preening book, written out of some misguided notion that subjectivity is truth. Bill Cole's *John Coltrane* (1976), though superior to Thomas's book, suffers from a similar problem.... [T]o explain Coltrane's spiritual life and his involvement with African and Asian culture, Cole merely grafts on the thought of African composer and music theorist Fela Sowande instead of exploring, or indeed even naming, the philosophical works Cole assures us that Coltrane was reading.... [T]he result is a book that reveals more about Cole's, rather than Coltrane's, encounter with African thought.[4]

In charting the influence of *A Love Supreme* beyond the context of the album's creation into other musical spheres and artistic and cultural contexts, two primary themes emerge that at first glance can appear diametrically opposed. On the one hand, the album is regarded as a marker of authenticity because it is linked explicitly to Coltrane's biography and personal quest and, more broadly, to the continuing legacy of black music. There is an ongoing strategy to promote Coltrane as speaking on behalf of African Americans, and, as Leonard Brown suggests, the artist was operating among a community "where you had to be invited," underlining its exclusivity of ownership and understanding.

On the other hand, *A Love Supreme* is treated as something universal, not tied to any particular people or place but a work that is drawn from a wealth of different influences. The work exudes themes of universal love and spirituality and is open and adaptable. This enables the work to be absorbed by different cultural groups, from hippies to rock musicians, as the music is seen to resonate with universal themes that bring people together. This hybrid, ever-changing and all-encompassing universality can appear to be at odds with the authentic, which is presented as originary, concerned with lineage, focused, and accessible only to those with privileges and a sense of the "real." To demonstrate how these themes play out in the *A Love Supreme* narrative, I will provide examples of how the album is used as a vehicle to promote both authenticity and universality.

AUTHENTICITY

Although the concept of authenticity has been challenged and regarded as a mythic construct in critical and cultural studies research, *A Love Supreme* feeds into the desire for authenticity in jazz more than any other album. Today, the majority of writings and representations of *A Love Supreme* portray the album as something deeply personal, an intimate statement of Coltrane's devotion to God. The reverence and respect shown to Coltrane and his spiritual outpouring is testament to the power of *A Love Supreme* and the way the work moves beyond the status of a simple studio recording. For artists to contemplate performing tracks from *A Love Supreme* presents a particular challenge, not only musically but also ethically. By producing an album that is so heavily bound up with Coltrane's personal quest, it is easy to feel restricted by authenticity narratives: *A Love Supreme* promotes the notion that this is a truly original artwork that cannot be replicated or mimicked without somehow undermining the intentions of the artist and the context of the work's creation.

As Ashley Kahn argues, apart from Charles Lloyd's "Tribal Dance," which is a melodic derivative of "Resolution," there were no cover versions of *A Love Supreme* or individual movements from the suite during Coltrane's lifetime. Kahn continues: "Even after his demise, an apparent reluctance persisted...[T]he material might have been too tightly connected to Coltrane himself....Or perhaps it was just too soon."[5] From the 1970s on, tributes and cover versions of individual tracks would emerge. And yet, even at this time, complete reworkings of the album were still quite rare, especially when compared to the number of different types of remake associated with a seminal album such as *Kind of Blue*.[6] Even when reworkings and tributes did take place, they were usually presented as having a deep connection with Coltrane or as somehow embodying the spiritual values that permeated the album. These tributes ranged from Alice Coltrane's version of "Acknowledgement," titled "A Love Supreme" on her 1971 album *World Galaxy*, to the jazz-rock version of *A Love Supreme* (which also uses material from "Acknowledgement") featured on Carlos Santana and John McLaughlin's 1973 album *Love Devotion Surrender*. In Alice Coltrane's case, the familial links to Coltrane provide a suitable justification for the homage, whereas Santana and McLaughlin cite the monumental presence of Coltrane and the spiritual catharsis that can be achieved in performing this work: McLaughlin portrayed performing the piece as a "liberating act," whereas Santana describes the way in which the music can make musicians feel "like they have the Holy Spirit in them."[7] Subsequent tributes continued in this vein, with the ever-present power of the Coltrane legacy shaping interpretations and the limits of re-creation. Even when Classic Quartet members produced their versions of sections of the suite, there remained a feeling of tampering with something sacred, as saxophonist Frank Foster stressed after his performance with Elvin Jones, "I wish I had stuck to my guns and said, 'No, Elvin, I can't do this.'"[8]

Come the 1990s, and over 25 years after Coltrane's death, different types of musical tribute began to emerge, and different artists chose to cover or reference the album more frequently. From this period, several musicians produced reworkings of individual movements from the work and a few recorded their own versions of the suite in its entirety. Despite the range of broader musical interpretations, the need to authenticate individual versions of the suite continued to unite the artists who tackled Coltrane's masterwork. Indeed, as *A Love Supreme* continues to become more canonical, the more artists feel the weight of the

Coltrane legacy and the sense that the album is a sacred work that must not be tampered with. As Ravi Coltrane argues, "To me, it's sacred as a whole. *A Love Supreme* is not just a tune or a record, it's an offering to God, and not just an idle offering."[9] Ravi Coltrane's evaluation is that *A Love Supreme* is a sacred and highly personalized statement.

The impact of this form of sacralization can be found in the references to authenticity in the statements of artists who have recorded *A Love Supreme* in its entirety. For example, Branford Marsalis reworked the suite as part of his *Footsteps of Our Fathers* album in 2002; Marsalis recognized the symbolic importance of *A Love Supreme* and was quoted as saying that he couldn't emulate the work of Coltrane. In his approach to playing the final movement, "Psalm," he states, "To me, that's Coltrane's personal statement, his personal improvisation. I don't even try to duplicate that."[10] Despite Marsalis's acknowledgment that Coltrane's original is a deeply personal statement that cannot be surpassed, the liner notes to the album—written by Delfayo Marsalis—frame Marsalis's interpretation of *A Love Supreme* in contrast to inauthentic Coltrane imitators:

> All too often, the performers who are credited as "Coltrane clones," or "owing a debt to Coltrane," actually don't play like Coltrane at all. First and foremost, Coltrane was a highly spiritual man. A clone would have to absorb comparative cultural experiences—which are virtual impossible to replicate in our current society—and translate the resultant emotions into musical expression.[11]

Coltrane's music is described as unsurpassable and impossible to absorb in today's cultural conditions, but the liner notes go on to single out Branford Marsalis as a musician who is capable of engaging with Coltrane on a spiritual as well as a technical level. Marsalis is an artist who exposes his contemporaries for what they are: inauthentic, academically motivated, and technically obsessed Coltrane imitators. The liner notes continue to differentiate Marsalis from his peers by describing the way in which the artist sounds "equally like and unlike John Coltrane," as if to demonstrate both Marsalis's intimate connection to Coltrane *and* his own original voice. These authenticating statements continue to invest in the legitimacy of *A Love Supreme*—this is no radical departure from Coltrane's original—at the same time as placing Branford Marsalis as a modern-day master firmly rooted in the continuum of jazz history. Essentially, Marsalis is a contemporary artist capable of walking in the path of Coltrane and continuing the legacy. From the text of the liner note alone, Marsalis becomes the torchbearer for the spiritual jazz life, the blues tradition, and the ongoing sensibilities of African American people.

Themes of spirituality, continuity and tradition, love and hope, and race and authenticity have become clear interrelated themes associated with *A Love Supreme*. Most versions of the suite, or its individual movements, have attempted to capture one or more of these attributes in some way. Coltrane's own poetic message that accompanies the album and is used for the final movement, "Psalm," serves to conflate words and music and, in many respects, encourages others to do the same, asserting meaning above and beyond the musical sound world. When coupled with this initial confluence of words and music, subsequent decades of tributes and writings have helped to create hagiographic depictions of Coltrane and his music. Alongside the range of musical tributes, the presence of Coltrane—and *A Love Supreme*—as an influence in African American poetry has arguably done as much, if not more, to develop overarching Coltrane tropes than musical discourses. The void created by Coltrane's death was felt not just in musical circles.

Indeed, just as the artist had been turned into a folk hero among poets and intellectuals, his untimely death sparked a wave of introspection, questioning, and a search for meaning that was evidenced in several key works of poetry. Since Coltrane's death, the "Coltrane poem" has emerged as a distinct genre category, with the artist and his music being used as a vehicle to explore themes that are regarded as core to African American experience. Kimberly Benston's *Performing Blackness: Enactments of African-American Modernism* provides a detailed analysis of Coltrane poems and the changing cultural contexts in which they emerge. Benston discusses the way in which Coltrane's absence had a symbolic quality that was used by poets to explore themes such as the loss of voice in America, the alienation of black subjects, and the problem of historical containment. Within this context, Coltrane became a figure bound intimately to the defining and redefining of black authenticity. Poets sought to reclaim Coltrane as an act of remembering (and re-membering, as Benston suggests), with the blues serving as a unifying theme. Coltrane's death is treated as both a tragedy and a means of rebirth: it generates a mythic presence that can empower and transform. Benston addresses the reclamation and birth of the mythic "Trane":

> The propelling recovery of an authentic self depends upon a reclamation
> of time, language, and finally, of Coltrane "himself." The dead must be

transformed into an instrument of the living imagination whereby the poet and his people can assess their mission in a new way. The resultant metamorphosis of Coltrane into "Trane," of figure into figuration, tells a story central to the evolution of modern African-American poetics as it reshapes the values of culture, history, and poetry itself. The death of Coltrane ultimately becomes in modern black poetry an event not of communal recession but of cultural redefinition.[12]

Through Coltrane, African American experience is reimagined, and notions of loss, death, and containment play off against themes of empowerment, rebirth, and freedom. Throughout, Coltrane is reborn as a powerful presence, a symbol of renewal and the authenticity of African American experience.

For poets, Coltrane's music provided a perfect vehicle for exploring the performative aspects of their art, and *A Love Supreme*, in particular, presented poets with an inspirational benchmark, a landmark recording that demonstrates the way in which music and poetry can be conflated. The album also offered itself as an ideal model of spiritualized blackness, with themes of rebirth, triumph over adversity, unbounded love, and unmediated expression contributing to the power and impact of the music on poets. For example, look at the following short excerpt from Sonia Sanchez's *a/coltrane/poem*:

> yrs befo u blew away our passsst
> and showed us our futureeeeee
> screech screech screeeeech screeech
> a/love/supreme, alovesupreme a lovesupreme.
> A LOVE SUPREME
> scrEEEccCHHHHH screeeeEEECHHHHHHHHHH
> SCREEEEEEEEECCCHHHHHHHHHHHHHHHHHH
> a lovesupremelovesupremelovesupreme for our blk
> people.[13]

This example illustrates quite clearly how performance is integral to the structure of the Coltrane poem. The text not only creates a sense of Coltrane's music in the scanning and structure of the poem, it also employs quotation and song, from *A Love Supreme* to *My Favorite Things*. The poem is articulated rhythmically and involves both bodily and oratory instruction, from whispers to the stamping of feet. The performative dimension of the poem mirrors jazz performance, in the sense that the reader/speaker takes on the guise of performer, with the poet giving over narrative control and owner-ship to the delivery of the text "in the moment." Indeed, Benston suggests that the conception of the poem as a situated performance event means that an authentic reading of the poem can never be rehearsed, it must be performed and shaped in performance for a specific context.[14] The poem is delivered on the edge, conjuring up the feeling of "liveness" and spontaneity experienced in a Coltrane performance. The success of *a/coltrane/poem* comes in its ability not only to imitate and recreate the performative aspects of Coltrane's music but also in its ability to reimagine Coltrane, moving from imitation to appropriation and transformation.

By exploring Coltrane from one's own performative context or embodying Coltrane, Sanchez and other Coltrane poets transform Coltrane into a political figure who serves as an agent for change. Whether this worldview was shared by Coltrane during his lifetime is irrelevant. The birth of "Trane" as a martyred prophet serves as a vehicle for galvanizing black authenticity, reifying notions of collective consciousness, a totalized history, and enhances the prospects of an essential nationhood. Transforming Coltrane into Trane through embodied performance heightens the impact of the message; the poem has a corporeal quality that serves as a textual and physical vehicle for political activism. Simultaneously, by using Trane as a type of medium, the performance encourages a reimagining of Coltrane's life and music: *A Love Supreme* turns into both spiritual and political statement, and the artist's untimely death becomes a call to arms. The performative value of the poem is enhanced by the political context as Coltrane is used as a signifier of empowerment; blackness is defiant, and Coltrane shows us how to live in the face of white capitalist oppression. The process of borrowing from Coltrane to live out one's own values and ambitions could be interpreted as in the same way as Tucker's critique of J. C. Thomas and Bill Cole mentioned earlier.[15] Furthermore, the continual remythologizing of Coltrane in this way has an inevitable impact on our reading of the artist and his place in history: through poetry, Coltrane is remembered through the prism of an idealized authentic blackness.

Beyond Sanchez's work, several Coltrane poems draw on *A Love Supreme* as a thematic device, although no poet has referred to Coltrane, or the album, as intently as Michael Harper. Coltrane formed an important part of Harper's cultural upbringing. His long-standing meditation on the life and works of the jazz icon has been interpreted as a way for Harper to reflect on himself as an artist and the enduring qualities of black culture more generally.[16] One of Harper's most famous poems,

Dear John Dear Coltrane (1970), uses *A Love Supreme* as a structural and symbolic reference point. The poem deals with extremities of the African American experience, moving from themes of slavery, loss, and dismemberment to a sense of eternal resolve, enduring presence, and spirituality. Functioning as a kind of elegy for Coltrane, the poem blends textual descriptions of Coltrane's physical decline with symbolic accounts of loss and fragmentation that have been read as the defining features of African American life.[17] Through Coltrane, Harper explores the stark imagery of decay, pain, and loss, alongside the manipulation and exploitation of black subjects through time. However, the presence of Coltrane, and continual return to *A Love Supreme*, enables the poet to contrast these oppressive themes with a vision of hope and eternal quality. As Benston states, "Coltrane approaches unavoidable death as a return to the primal trope of affirmation, 'a love supreme,' that love of the self which endures in spite and because of all that has been taken, all that has been given in suffering."[18] Within the context of the poem, Coltrane lives on despite the acts of dismemberment and physical decay to become a powerful emblem of liberation and transcendence. This is a metaphor for the African American tradition: the continual suffering that has formed an essential part of the African American past continues to form a part of modern experiences, but can be overcome through performative acts and spiritual renewal.

Harper has described his own poetry as a type of jazz, its shifting moods aligned to different modalities, and has cited that the influence of Coltrane is central to his dramatic prose.[19] Paralleling Coltrane's use of musical modality, Harper's modality offers an explanation for a way of living that is embodied in the life force of Coltrane:

"By modality I mean the creation of an environment so intense by its life and force as to revivify and regenerate, spiritually, man and community...out of such energy comes community and freedom. A Love Supreme!"[20]

Harper's desire to create a synergy between poetry and jazz has also manifested itself in performance projects that blend music with poetry. In his 2004 recording *Double Take: Jazz-Poetry Conversations*, for example, Harper performs several Coltrane poems in duet with Paul Austerlitz.[21] Harper's performance of *Brother John*—which also draws reference to *A Love Supreme*—offers a good example of the musical qualities of Harper's work, as the performance brings out the concepts of tension and release, the intensity of repetition and fluid feel of improvisation. Austerlitz's stylistic changes mirror Harper's changes in content—moving among stylized improvisations that echo Bird, Miles, and Coltrane—and yet, the music serves only to accentuate the way in which the text functions as music, itself taking on the stylistic attributes of different iconic jazzmen.

Coltrane poems, although different in their use and engagement with Coltrane, have served as a clear example of the way in which musical influence extends beyond sonic boundaries. Poets have drawn on *A Love Supreme* as a cultural touchstone that resonates among the African American community. As a marker of authenticity, *A Love Supreme* enables poets to reimagine the world and interrogate concepts of self and other, oppression and liberation, through the mythic transformation of Coltrane.

Although Coltrane poems provide the most overt references to *A Love Supreme*, the album has also been used more abstractly in African American literature. For example, Lars Eckstein uses *A Love Supreme* as an analytical tool to uncover what he describes as "jazzthetic" strategies in the literature of African American writer Toni Morrison. By comparing the novel *Beloved* to *A Love Supreme*, Eckstein does not concern himself with overt musical references in Morrison's text or, indeed, whether the author was influenced explicitly by the seminal album in creating her work. Instead, he explores the way in which Morrison's writing comes to embody black music and articulates ideas that are central to African American experience: "Morrison *musicalizes* her fiction: she charts the origins and traditions of jazz in her particular choice of characters. On a structural level, she carefully incorporates aspects of the formal arrangement of jazz, and pragmatically, she makes use of the performative and expressive scope of black music."[22] This suggests that jazz music—and *A Love Supreme* in particular—can be seen to embody values and techniques that are central to understanding African American life. This ranges from the way in which jazz techniques such as call and response, improvisation, and blues themes are found in the writing style of Morrison, to a more abstract idea of the way music gives voice to the inherent sense of loss, or, as Paul Gilroy discusses, "the condition of pain" in black music.[23]

Eckstein compares passages of *Beloved* to the unfolding musical discourse of *A Love Supreme* as if to suggest Morrison adopts a musical strategy in the development of her work. He continues:

The placement of *Beloved* in the realm of African American music is Morrison's key to overcoming the speechlessness of trauma and to engaging in a constructive dialogue with painful chapters of the past. The broken beats of the blues, spirituals, and jazz that the novel takes up are so firmly rooted in the African diaspora that they establish a secure foundation for the exploration of suffering and pain.[24]

Despite these essentializing statements and the romanticized commitment to Gilroy's "ethics of antiphony," Coltrane's *A Love Supreme* is posited as the quintessential musical model for understanding African American experience.[25] As Eckstein suggests, the suite is representative of a larger genus of African American musical styles. He argues that the qualities that the music embodies straddle music contexts and everyday life, and, as such, *A Love Supreme* is regarded as an authentic statement of African American experience. As music, the suite blends African, Afro-Christian and secular traditions within a unifying aesthetic of spirituality, and the blues becomes a central concept that underpins black experience. *A Love Supreme* promotes a sense of collectivity—or the blending of voices—as well as the creativity of improvisation, and Eckstein argues that these are the qualities that Morrison is seen to explore through the characters in *Beloved*. Morrison's text, like Coltrane's suite, does not encourage an opposition between western and African styles but, instead, demonstrates the power of black culture to integrate and adjust to the changing conditions of American experience.

I would argue that, when taken as a whole, the musical tributes, Coltrane poems, and uses of *A Love Supreme* in literary contexts demonstrate the way in which Coltrane and his music have become a cornerstone for articulating African American experience. Coltrane and his music are often related to notions of collective consciousness, a linear past, continuity, innate links to Africa that support the idea of an essential blackness. Whether this is real or imagined, the concept of essential blackness continues to serve as a powerful agent in asserting African American identity. Coltrane's life, music, and, more important, myth, become an important component in engendering a sense of authentic blackness. *A Love Supreme* has developed as the archetypal signifier of the core values of the African American tradition. Despite the multitude of influences and significations and, indeed, the number of Coltrane mythologies and remythologies that emerged both within and beyond his lifetime, a certain reification has occurred where Coltrane and his music become associated with overarching tropes and cultural practices: themes of spirituality, tradition, honesty, purity, triumph over adversity, and politicization converge to the point where they become interchangeable with the idea of Coltrane himself.

There are real dangers in recent representations of indigenous peoples in popular discourse, and especially in the media, which stress claims to an "authentic" voice. For these claims, by overwriting the actual complexity of difference may write out that voice as effectively as earlier oppressive discourses of reportage. In fact, it may well be the same process at work.[26]

Though it can be argued that Coltrane helped end jazz's mass popularity with his expressionistic, visceral approach to music, his own appeal and influence was immense, reaching way beyond the confines of jazz or even music[27]

Universality is the second major narrative theme to emerge from the range of writings and representations of *A Love Supreme*. In several respects, as discussed earlier, the concept of universality can be viewed in opposition to authenticity. For example, if a work's meaning is understood by all then it cannot be claimed only by select groups who seek to promote an authentic reading of a work or claim a unique or exclusive relationship with it. As with notions of authenticity, promoting a sense of universality in music is deeply problematic, and represents a common romantic trope tied into the description of jazz practices. Indeed, the idea of jazz music being a "universal language" is a well-trodden mythology that continues to be promoted by artists and audiences alike. These types of understanding do not engage with the cultural specificity of works of art and the way in which they are born out of particular circumstances and, inevitably, reinforce depictions of music as autonomous, transcendent, and immune to social and cultural influence. Janet Wolff, for example, has been a strong advocate for a social reading of art where notions of universality are redundant. Rather than viewing art as universal, transcendent and uniform, Wolf states: "Works of art, on the contrary, are not closed, self-contained and transcendent entities, but are the product of specific historical practices on the part of identifiable social groups in given conditions, and therefore bear the imprint of the ideas, values and conditions of existence of those groups, and their representatives in particular artists."[28]

Applying this to Coltrane, I argue that the concept of universality does not deal with the fact that works come to mean different things to different people depending on the time, context, or particular values they bring to the listening experience. Or, indeed, they do not account for the ways in which Coltrane's music has accrued a range of different meanings over time. Despite these reservations, however, when Coltrane went on record, he tended to promote a universal aesthetic, both in terms of his spiritual outlook and his obsessive interest in understanding the different musics of the world. In Coltrane's last interview with Frank Kofsky, for example, he discussed the need to appeal to different audiences, both black and white, and to draw on a range of cultures from Europe to Africa to Asia.[29] Building on this, Ravi Coltrane describes his father's music as "striving for a universal language through sound, using his music as a connecting force, trying to call together the most basic and divine qualities that are common to all human experience."[30]

In contrast to the authenticity narratives that have engulfed interpretations of *A Love Supreme*, it is important to explore ways in which the album has influenced a broad spectrum of cultural practices. Both during and beyond Coltrane's lifetime, *A Love Supreme* has been taken on by, appropriated, and influenced a whole range of artists, from rock musicians to novelists and filmmakers. The appeal of the work stems from Coltrane's own openness to new ideas as well as the feeling that the suite has something profound to say about all humanity. In this respect, universality does not necessarily tie into a shared meaning and common mode of understanding but can be used as a means of exploring how certain themes emerge from the suite that have been used, albeit differently, in a variety of contexts. Since the release of *A Love Supreme*, the album has come to represent a host of meanings tied to broad themes of love and universal spirituality. This breadth of meaning, and the album's ability to appeal to different interests, is a significant factor in the ongoing success of the album and its cross-cultural appeal. Despite the power of Coltrane as an iconic figure that serves as a marker of authenticity for the neo-traditionalist mainstream, I would suggest that Coltrane's influence can be seen as more widespread than this relatively narrow field. Ben Ratliff, for example, has described how neo-traditionalism and Coltrane's output are not necessarily compatible, as the artist drew on a range of influences to support the development of his music and wasn't concerned with constructing history in a linear and compartmentalized manner. In many ways, Coltrane's music could be seen as divisive, countering the desire to construct a homogenous tradition. And yet, figures such as Branford and Wynton Marsalis have sought to champion the music of Coltrane at points within their career, controlling the artist's representation to suit their own values and musical preferences. I will return to Wynton Marsalis's interpretation of *A Love Supreme* later.

First, consider the following statement by Ratliff: "Since his death it has taken jazz musicians more than thirty years to find a consensual, mainstream language of rapprochement between free jazz and the more traditionally based kind."[31] Ratliff's comments touch upon the types of cultural transformations and negotiations that have taken place in the years following Coltrane's death. Indeed, the shared meanings and consensual understandings of the artist's contribution to jazz history have taken time to emerge to the point where common themes and narrative tropes are now widespread. The contrast between authenticity tropes and themes of universality demonstrate the way in which Coltrane's persona and *A Love Supreme* are malleable, adapted to suit particular contexts and cultural narratives. For example, Ratliff describes the way in which Coltrane's representation feeds into a range of narrative models and cites the contrasting character traits of the spirit-filled archetype of West African Congo culture with depictions of Coltrane that cast him as the Yankee woodsman or a John Wayne–type figure. Building on this, I would suggest that different manifestations of Coltrane's character feed into mythic representations supporting underlying authentic belief systems: artists can be cowboys as well as saints, as their mediated images and biographies change according to the particular cultural values being supported at any given time. Although a number of representations of Coltrane have emerged since his death, the rise in the canonical status of jazz has intensified the focus on the spiritual aspects of Coltrane's music. This has led to a dominant representation of the artist as a force for good in which he has, literally, been transformed into a saint.

By contrast, the aesthetic of the frontier and the musician as pioneer or outlaw has been discussed by several writers.[32] In particular, during the 1960s, the concept of the musician as outlaw or pioneer manifested itself in several forms, from the experimental sounds of New Black Music to the anarchy and hedonism of rock music. Michael Jarrett describes the synergy between jazz and rock aesthetics during this period: "Rock mythology had followed a trail blazed by jazz. The quest for a unique sound, a privileging of invention over interpretation, an infatuation with drugs, sex, and spirituality: Both musics glorified an ideology founded on individualism."[33] The Coltrane biography and appeal of *A Love Supreme* tie into many of these traits. As Coltrane's most spiritual and individual work, the album can appeal to audiences who are not necessarily interested in jazz and is often presented as a work of original conception, the result of Coltrane's obsession with creating a unique sound. Whereas rock music might have created a synergy between drugs, experimentation, and ecstasy (as we can read into Coltrane's late works), *A Love Supreme* presents the listener with a narrative of purity and the negative impact of drug addiction: it is a heroic, almost biblical, story of triumph over adversity and devotion to God, and conveys the idea of universal principles. Although the representation of Coltrane shares a lot of common traits with rock music, the widespread popularity of Coltrane's unabashed devotion to God in *A Love Supreme* could be seen as surprising in the context of a rock and pop culture that was often presented as antithetical to religion. One needs to think only of the outrage caused by John Lennon's 1966 statement "We're more popular than Jesus" or the way in which, over several decades, musicians (such as Cliff Richard) have been ridiculed for outward bursts of Christian zeal. And yet, spirituality and mysticism remain core elements of the experimental mood of the times and the success of *A Love Supreme*'s overt religious offering could be understood more widely when looking to other jazz and classical works of the period.[34]

Musically, *A Love Supreme* has appealed to a much wider constituency of artists than the authenticity narratives suggest. Take, for example, American minimalists such as La Monte Young and Steve Reich. Despite producing musical sound worlds radically different from Coltrane, composers such as Young have cited Coltrane as a major influence in thinking about the cosmic potential of music, how sound relates to concepts of philosophy, nature, and spiritual ideals.[35] Equally, Reich has discussed the significant influence of Coltrane on his own career development, charting Coltrane's interest in African music and his works on Impulse up until *A Love Supreme* as the main factor in convincing him to change his own approach to composition.[36] Reich's music has drawn on a range of cultural influences, and the composer's own desire to study African drumming was influenced by the openness expressed in Coltrane's music to draw on new cultures. Although the link between *A Love Supreme* and American minimalism operates mainly at the conceptual and symbolic level, the drone-like, modal qualities of the music coupled with the concepts of repetition, minor variation and timelessness relate directly to Coltrane's own experiments of the mid-1960s. In Reich's case, beyond the overarching influence, interest in African culture and conceptual approaches to music, there are resonances of the compositional devices of *A Love Supreme* in the cell structures of the composer's work, most notably his *Six Pianos* written in 1973. Taken together with Reich's previous discussion of the impact of Coltrane on his development, it is clear that the influence of Coltrane and *A Love Supreme* transcends genre.

This is also evidenced in the Turtle Island String Quartet's arrangement of the suite, placing *A Love Supreme* firmly in the realm of art music. Although the string quartet's reworking of Coltrane's magnum opus lacks the vibrancy, rhythmic complexity, and spontaneity of the

Classic Quartet's, the arrangement does serve to highlight the composed elements of the suite. When compared to the other tracks on the string quartet's album, *A Love Supreme* offers itself as the most convincing arrangement, moving beyond the mere novelty of instrumentation change and contextual connotation (from jazz to classical music) toward a reworking that illustrates through sound, the changing status of Coltrane's masterwork.

A Love Supreme's ability to promote themes of universal spirituality is perhaps best illustrated in Kurt Elling's vocalese version of Coltrane's "Resolution." Elling sets words both to Coltrane's "Resolution" theme, and to his improvised solo, which evoke different faiths, drawing on religious figures, gods, and prophets ranging from Buddha to Allah, Vishnu to Jesus in order to convey a sense of deeper meaning to life and enlightenment through spirituality. Within different cultural contexts, references to *A Love Supreme* have become shorthand for promoting the idea of universal spirituality. The mere mention of Coltrane as an inspiration or reference to *A Love Supreme* as a seminal influence connotes a particular artistic and spiritual sensitivity. Pop musician Bono, for example, cited *A Love Supreme* as a significant influence and even included a fleeting reference to the suite in U2's 1988 track "Angel of Harlem." Also in 1988, singer-songwriter Will Downing's track "A Love Supreme" imitated Coltrane's chant as a chorus to the song. Produced with the consent of Alice Coltrane, Downing's "A Love Supreme" focuses on the contentment of finding love but also draws reference to having faith in God.

More recently, references to Coltrane's seminal work within popular culture have not only followed the themes of universal love and spirituality but have also appeared more abstract, bound up with nostalgia for the 1960s and sounds of a particular time and place. Robbie Williams's "Supreme" from the 2000 album *Sing When You're Winning*, combines the lyrical chant "A Love Supreme" with samples from Gloria Gaynor's hit "I Will Survive." The track's music video evokes the past by superimposing Williams onto archival footage from the late 1960s to early 1970s, and creating a fictional story line that sets Williams as a Formula One racing driver against real-life racing legend Jackie Stewart. When exploring the Coltrane influence as part of this product, the reference to *A Love Supreme* might appear vague and tenuous, to say the least. Indeed, the words "A Love Supreme" might have as much to do with referencing Will Downing as they do Coltrane. However, I argue that this is significant as it demonstrates the way in which the album has permeated popular culture to become an ever-changing signifier. When examining Williams's "Supreme" in relation to Coltrane's suite, it is possible to understand *A Love Supreme* as a type of broad-based sign of the 1960s, both a nostalgia trope for a bygone era and a means of dealing with conflicts of the present day. Williams's lyrics include "This new century keeps bringing you down.... Come and live a love supreme." Here, *A Love Supreme* offers a metaphorical escape from the present, a means of finding love and contentment away from the corruption of today.

In broader cultural contexts, the evocation of *A Love Supreme* often feeds into an array of related themes linked to truth, honesty, devotion, and a more general faith, although themes may play out in different ways. Kent Nussey's 2003 novel *A Love Supreme*, subsequently made into a film by Bruce McDonald, uses Coltrane's music as a central narrative device that helps the central character to overcome the anxieties of his personal life and find love. By contrast, Paolo Parisi's recent graphic novel *Coltrane* uses *A Love Supreme* as a central structural device to tell the story of Coltrane's life with fictional embellishments. Using artwork and quotes from different interviews with Coltrane, Parisi constructs a biographical text in which the main markers and myths of Coltrane's career are conveyed pictorially. The narrative is nonchronological and flits between the key moments of Coltrane's career, blending scenes and imagined conversations from Coltrane's personal life with accounts of Coltrane's seminal recordings. As a graphic novel, the highly stylized storyboard-style narrative is a demonstration of cross-disciplinary creative practice. Parisi develops creative content from Coltrane's music, key interviews (most notably Coltrane's conversation with Frank Kofsky), and Lewis Porter's biography of the artist, using sound and text as the starting point for his artwork. Parisi states that the layout of the book "immediately creates the structure of the [*A Love Supreme*] album: four chapters to the book, four parts to the album. In one sense, the idea is to connect the reading to the listening."[37] Each of the four chapters is named after a section of the suite.

The use of Coltrane's suite as a signifier of truth and honesty has also been taken up by advertisers. The New York–based company Supreme was launched in 2004 and has become an important fashion house for the skater community and, more generally, a broad-based artistic street style. Endorsements of the company have come from a wide range of artists and celebrities, including Damien Hurst and Lady Gaga. In 2009, the company featured a 16-minute film titled *A Love Supreme* on its website that was underscored by "Acknowledgement" and "Resolution" from Coltrane's suite.[38] The black-and-white film focuses on skaters in

New York and moves through a range of sequences that connects differ-ent shots of skaters to community groups and the urban landscape; Coltrane's suite is linked not only to the successful brand but also to New York and its related jazz scene. *A Love Supreme* can be interpreted as music of the street; it is urban, honest, and in touch with people. Furthermore, the music also serves to promote the values of community and collectivity, themes that are ever-present within the film and the marketing strategies of the Supreme brand. Within the film, the virtu-osity and performativity of the Classic Quartet is also projected onto the New York skaters, as their tricks and stunts are enhanced dramati-cally by the music, mirroring the sophistication and creativity of the sounds on record. The film provides a good example of the complex sig-nifiers at play when encountering *A Love Supreme* in a remediated envi-ronment, from the album's integral links to jazz history to nostalgia for the 1960s, from tying the music to the urban landscape of New York to more amorphous values such as belonging, sensuality, hipness, and a feeling of being in touch with the times, the vernacular spirit of the here and now. As the suite has gained in canonical status, the performative aspects of the album could be lost or downplayed as the suite is cele-brated for its cerebral qualities, its sense of spiritual uplift and meta-physical qualities. Therefore, projects that engage with Coltrane's music visually and physically, like the Supreme film, help to restore some of the performative dimension to the music, providing the disembodied sounds of Coltrane with a renewed physical presence.[39]

Another project that highlights the physical dimension of *A Love Supreme* is Anna Teresa de Keersmaeker and the Belgian Rosas dance ensemble's 2005 production *Raga for the Rainy Season/A Love Supreme*, a choreographed work that juxtaposes the Classic Quartet's original recording with Indian ragas. The spiritual connection between Coltrane and Indian ragas formed part of the concept for the work, and, though themes of spirituality are present, the use of Coltrane's music in this context is far removed from the suite's original context. By turning Coltrane's seminal work into a choreographed piece, de Keersmaeker adds a new dimension to the work, enabling new meanings and inter-pretations to emerge.[40]

CHALLENGING ESTABLISHED NARRATIVES

While narratives of authenticity and universalism dominate portrayals of *A Love Supreme*, distinctions between these themes are not always

Figure 4.1:
Flyer: Opening of Olatunji Center of African Culture, Harlem, NYC, April 23, 1967.
Photo by Norman Saks courtesy of Yasuhiro "Fuji" Fujioka Collection.

clear. Indeed, examples exist in which authenticity and universalism are merged, sidestepped, or transformed into different cultural contexts. To illustrate this, consider the different ways in which the African influence has been picked up in previous writings on jazz and the music of John Coltrane.[41] Musician Randy Weston has described the way in which the music of Coltrane has a universal quality that ties directly into the sounds of African communities:

> I've been listening extensively to African folklore music from the Congo, from Nigeria, from Ghana, from Morocco, and the more I listen to this music, the more I'm influenced by it, the more I realize that it contains the elements of all the musical forms of modern Africa and the New World.... I've heard cats who sound just like Coltrane. The music of the tribes is just unbelievable.[42]

Despite Weston's attempts to demonstrate the relationship between Africa and jazz, most writings on the subject have a tendency to describe the African influence in mystical and ancient terms, presenting the continent as a remote ancestral home for African American jazz musicians. While these types of representation serve to support the easily digestible view of jazz history as a "changing same," the depiction of Africa as an ancient land inevitably contributes to African American exceptionalist readings of history that, in turn, devalue the interplay between jazz and African society today. In many respects, Coltrane's fascination with African, as well as Asian and European, musics offered a powerful alternative to the view of jazz history as being self contained within the American continent.

Indeed, through Coltrane's work, there was as much fascination with the African past as there was with the African present, and Coltrane's African-themed music and endorsements of the work of Babatunde Olatunji, for example, provided examples of the artist's desire to find value in musics from around the world, to connect with African cultures and to engage with current musical scenes. The connection to Africa was evidenced in the title of several of Coltrane's compositions, and the artist also expressed a desire to visit Africa to gather musical materials.[43] Furthermore, Coltrane's headline appearance at the "Roots of Africa" concert to launch the Olatunji Center of African Culture in 1967 was also a powerful sign of support for the celebration and preservation of African culture in the United States.

The legacy of this work, and Coltrane's commitment to discovery, is something that has triggered a powerful following for Coltrane in a range of international settings. Steven Feld's *Jazz Cosmopolitanism in Accra* offers a compelling example of the cultural influence *A Love Supreme* and Coltrane's late music today. During Feld's trip to Ghana, the late music of Coltrane, and *A Love Supreme* in particular, became the catalyst for a remarkable journey that enabled Feld to engage more deeply with cultural life in Accra. Through a shared enthusiasm for the music of Coltrane, Feld embarked on an intense period of conversations, performances, collaborations, and recording projects that enabled him to gain insights into the transnational character of music making today. In this, the authenticity and universality narratives of *A Love Supreme* converged in a complex example of cosmopolitanism in jazz, examining not only the American influence internationally but also the ways in which music means different things in different contexts, facilitates exchanges between people, and questions straightforward assumptions of musical influence. Consider the words of Feld's Ghanaian collaborator Nii Noi, who describes the idea of using Coltrane as the central influence for his Accra Train Station project:

> Well, Accra Train Station—Coltrane Station is interesting because the music of Coltrane is universal and Accra has always served as the Pan-African capital. So Accra embracing Coltrane is part of the historical process. Accra becomes the new focus for John Coltrane. In other words, Coltrane has finally arrived in Africa. It's no longer just a dream on records and on titles, but now it's a real acceptance of the man's works in Africa[44]

Here, Coltrane's universalism is combined with authenticity narratives: he is finally accepted in Africa, claimed as part of African culture. This process is far from straightforward and illustrates the power and dynamics of cultural influence, transfer, and exchange. Within this context, Coltrane's late music and African-themed pieces encourage African musicians to celebrate their cultural identity. Paradoxically, as music that, in many respects, presents an imagined picture of Africa, Coltrane's music is translated back into African life, encouraging African musicians to feel *more* African. This example not only demonstrates how Coltrane is assimilated and appropriated in different international settings and how his music epitomizes a form of jazz cosmopolitanism, but it also shows how African musicians use Coltrane's late music to envisage a future for their own creativity and to celebrate their place in the world. This rides against straightforward or unidirectional descriptions of cultural influence that dominate typical interpretations of jazz history.

CHANGING PERCEPTIONS OF THE PAST

When listening to *A Love Supreme* today, there is a great temptation to think of the reception of the suite as unchanged over time, as if the music has retained the same meaning for over 40 years. Indeed, accounts of the album that depict *A Love Supreme* as a personal endeavor, the product of honest expression, and representative of the core values of Coltrane and the Classic Quartet support this view of history as unchanging through time. However, as the foregoing examples illustrate, meanings, themes, and overarching narrative tropes have developed over time to the point where the seminal album has gained a monumental place within the canon of recorded jazz. By appearing as unchanged through time, and embodying values that are both universal yet rooted in the essence of the African American tradition, the work offers itself as the perfect vehicle for promoting the values of the neo-traditionalist mainstream and, more generally, the enduring qualities of black culture in the United States.

Overall, however, the central themes and language of *A Love Supreme* manage to straddle different interest groups and provide a means of access or a type of cultural resonance that is simultaneously bound up with the 1960s and perceived as timeless: the album is tied to a specific social context and, paradoxically, set free of time. Whether *A Love Supreme* is understood as an authentic masterpiece, music with universal qualities, or as a recording whose influence has infiltrated the worlds of art, popular culture, literature, and dance, the album has resonated in different ways with a variety of groups and cultural contexts. Rather than favoring one interpretation of the work over others, these examples demonstrate how the album is polysemic: it has generated a web of complex meanings and associations since its release in 1965 to the point where, today, the album can be understood either as conveying a specific meaning (as Coltrane's sacred text) or as a broad-based cultural signifier. *A Love Supreme* can play with established boundaries between art and the vernacular. It can also be understood as a canonical jazz masterpiece at the same time as being a musical work with cross-genre appeal. The suite blends the experiences of the physical world with visions of the metaphysical: it is something deeply personal, and yet is widely understood to embody a collective spirit.

In spite of the plurality of meaning and widespread use of albums such as *A Love Supreme*, recordings have the power to generate specific mythologies and accrue dominant meanings over time. It is important to understand how *A Love Supreme* is used to promote particular values, the work being interpreted to suit particular ideological positions. Ideological control of Coltrane and *A Love Supreme* is clear in the rhetoric and actions of the Coltrane estate, ranging from Ravi Coltrane's description of the suite as something sacred that moves beyond the boundaries of jazz to the blocking of the use *A Love Supreme* as a title for Spike Lee's film (which later became *Mo' Better Blues*). These overt forms of ideological control, which echo hagiographic accounts of Coltrane's life and works, are perhaps overly cautious and dogmatic in approach yet are also understandable, given the desire among family members to preserve the sanctity of Coltrane's life and music. However, I argue that more subtle forms of ideological control surround *A Love Supreme*, as the album is used to promote particular values of different groups as well as a constructed view of the past. As an illustration of ideology in action, I want to consider three different uses of the album, each from the past 15 years but concentrating on different periods of history. By exploring how the album can work at the ideological level, it is possible to understand how recordings can alter interpretations and understandings of history. The three short examples include musicians and listener responses, as well as the broader cultural field within which *A Love Supreme* operates.

1. Lincoln Center Jazz Orchestra with Wynton Marsalis

A clear example of an ideologically motivated interpretation of *A Love Supreme* can be seen on the recording of Lincoln Center Jazz Orchestra with Wynton Marsalis's version of the suite, from 2004. In this reworking, the potential conflict between the themes of universality and authenticity is presented as being resolved within the structure of the music itself. This is Wynton Marsalis's interpretation of the meaning of the work as a type of journey: "The first thing is that he [Coltrane] has a cyclical form, which begins in the universal church and ends in the church of Negro spirituals.... The first movement ends with the congregation singing 'A Love Supreme.'... By the last movement, 'We are back in the church.' "[45] Marsalis portrays themes of universality and authenticity as part of a journey, a journey that ends with an affirmation of the values of the black church. Coltrane's chanting is interpreted as the sound of the congregation and his wide-ranging influences, from China to Latin America, form part of a narrative pathway to a homecoming, a return to the essential values of the African American tradition. Marsalis's interpretation does not directly conflict with other, more broad-based, interpretations of Coltrane's aesthetic that celebrate his music as a vast array of cultural influences.[46] Indeed, the breadth of influence is embraced as a sign of the music's sophistication. By concluding the work, "back in the church," however, Marsalis lays claim to

Coltrane as an authenticator of black experience: these are the values that conclude the work and sound out the collective consciousness of black America.

Marsalis's interpretation of the album differs slightly from his previous interpretations of Coltrane's suite. In an interview in 1990, Marsalis described the suite as being deeply spiritual but also stressed that the music has "an African polyphonic conception which is not like the church call and response, where somebody calls and somebody responds, but where calling and responding occur simultaneously."[47] The subtle changes in interpretation continue to root the work in African and African American conceptions, but the more recent description is more refined, signaling a specificity of influence and cultural place.

Stanley Crouch, who wrote the liner notes to the album, concludes with the following comments: "Nothing can ever replace the original, but, as this recording proves, even things we know about can be extended into areas beyond our imagination."[48] Within this context, "beyond our imagination" could easily serve as a euphemism for the ideological control of the Coltrane narrative: Coltrane's avant-gardism, experimental thinking, collective practice, and pluralism are cancelled out, as all roads lead back to asserting Coltrane as the hero of the neo-traditionalist mainstream. The ideological control of Coltrane is essential to the promotion of core values and beliefs bound up with the jazz tradition. Indeed, as an idealized iconic figure, Coltrane functions as the quintessential heroic figure as described by Albert Murray. Within the politics of American culture, Coltrane provides a powerful role model for African Americans, and the values and influence of A Love Supreme are obviously desirable for figures such as Marsalis who seek to demonstrate how jazz can move us to "higher ground."[49]

Despite this noble cause, using Coltrane to promote the positive contributions African American musicians have made to American culture more generally, the limited representation and interpretation of Coltrane in this context is problematic and, ultimately, essentializing. The brilliance of A Love Supreme comes in the album's ability to synthesize so many disparate sources and to appeal to a multitude of groups. If we adopt Marsalis's strategy and describe the suite conceptually as a type of journey, then it would miss the point to describe the album as a single voyage. Instead, the suite could be described as a multitude of journeys taken in a host of directions by many different people.

2. Rethinking *A Love Supreme*: The Alternate Takes

The second example of ideology in action focuses on the way in which *A Love Supreme* has become idealized to the extent where it changes our view of the past. The 2002 deluxe edition of Coltrane's suite features, for the first time, the Classic Quartet's December 9 recording alongside the alternate takes from the December 10 session. Although some of the material from the December session 10 remains lost, two sextet versions of "Acknowledgement," featuring Archie Shepp on tenor saxophone and Art Davis on bass, have been preserved. The fact that alternative session recordings have been available to the public only for the last 10 years creates a schism between the sounds of the original release and the alternative sextet versions that, inevitably, illustrate how history is often written and constructed retrospectively to reflect the values and needs of the present day. My comments here stem from my own experience of listening to *A Love Supreme* over many years and the way in which my relationship to the album has changed over time.

A Love Supreme's place, not only in the context of the 1960s but also as an object that resonates in American culture and beyond, becomes firmly embedded within our imaginations to the extent where the context of the work's creation becomes either remote and irrelevant to our listening experience or idealized and transformed into something mythic. In order to develop insights into ways in which different meanings have accrued over time, I would suggest listening to Coltrane tributes from the early 1970s—or, even better, the alternate takes from the *A Love Supreme* sessions—and consider the different ways in which we as listeners react to these alternative versions. For example, when listening to *Love, Devotion, Surrender* again after several years, the sincerity of Santana and McLaughlin's intentions expressed on this album, and the music's widespread popular appeal at the time, seemed at odds with the musical aesthetic of Coltrane's original. Indeed, listening with values of today and the way in which *A Love Supreme* has been idealized in my own mind, the jazz-rock version of the suite seemed overblown with its groove-based use of the *A Love Supreme* theme and its electric guitar sounds. This musical concept sounded dated and antithetical to the purity, artistic expression, and sanctity of Coltrane's original sound world as it is understood today.

With the sextet versions of "Acknowledgement," recorded on December 10, 1964, I argue that the material has the potential to create a seismic shift in our perception of the *A Love Supreme* sessions. My initial reaction on hearing the alternate takes was that, in many ways, the music sounded like an overdub (with Shepp's opening dialogue with Coltrane sounding like an intrusion) or like a completely new take, something far removed from our idea of the suite that has grown and emerged since the 1970s.

Even though the recordings were documented within a two-day period, the disjunction between the original recording and the recently released alternate takes demonstrates how history can skew our perceptions of the music. Hearing the alternate takes as something totally out of context demonstrate not only the freshness of the sound on record and the unfamiliarity of experience, but also the way in which the sounds of the original release have become fixed in our minds over time. I would go a stage further than this, however, and argue that our reception of the alternate takes can be affected by the power of ideology, which has manifested itself in reified conceptions of the suite. In many ways, listening to the alternate takes offers some of the most revealing insights into the mythmaking process and the way in which our listening experience becomes inseparable from the jazz narratives that surround works. I argue that the fact that the alternative takes sound *so* abrupt and shockingly out of context says more about the meanings that have accrued over time, and the symbolic quality of Coltrane's work, than they do about the music on record. Having access to material from the second recording date provides us with an opportunity to rethink

Figure 4.2:
John Coltrane at the *A Love Supreme* recording session, December 10, 1964. Courtesy of Photofest.

A Love Supreme and understand the way in which the work has been idealized since its release. By comparing our reactions to the alternate takes with our established idea of the original release, we can become aware of our own agency and involvement in the mythmaking process. Furthermore, as listeners, we become acutely aware of the power of recordings, their cultural influence and ability to change our perceptions of history.

The power of ideology, and idealized perspectives, is not just something that we as listeners experience. Archie Shepp's own retrospective response to his involvement in the album provides a powerful indication of the presence of ideology and its ability to alter our view of the past. When interviewed for Ashley Kahn's book in 2002, Shepp almost offers an apology for his contribution to the sessions: "Well, I wish I had listened more. When John does the intro, I think I'm completely off, I play something that doesn't sound at all related. If I had used my common sense, I would have played more—I didn't approach it as honestly as I should have because ['Acknowledgment'] is very beautiful, very plain, very minor."[50] Discussing his contribution to the *A Love Supreme* session in 2002, Shepp's reaction is clearly altered by the passage of time and the dominant representations of the suite that have emerged since the mid-1960s. Rather than challenging the hagiographic accounts of Coltrane's life and music and, indeed, the testimony of Classic Quartet members who played down the involvement of Shepp and Davis in order to preserve the sanctity of the original recording, Shepp discredits his own contribution, expressing the sense that he was daunted by the experience and on a completely different wavelength from Coltrane.[51]

Building on this, I would argue that, despite Shepp's modesty and sense of regret, these reactions to the alternate takes brings into focus the way in which the musical content of the album has been idealized over time. Indeed, I would suggest that Shepp and Davis's contributions to the second day of the *A Love Supreme* sessions are *not* poor, insignificant, or off the mark. For example, Coltrane discussed his decision to omit the sextet version in his interview with Michiel de Ruyter and stated that the only reason he did not include the second day takes was because he preferred the vocal chanting from the session on the first day.[52] Whether this is to be believed or not (and if it is, then Coltrane himself saw no significant reason why the second day's music should be omitted or considered substandard), a simple comparison of Shepp's contribution to *A Love Supreme* to his other, critically acclaimed recordings from the same period demonstrates a consistency of approach, invention, and tone: from Shepp's Impulse albums *Four for Trane* (1964) to his *Fire Music* (1965), the musical ideas and improvisations expressed on the *A Love Supreme* sessions are on a par with other projects at the time. If this is accepted, then the schism encountered between the original release and the *A Love Supreme* outtakes demonstrates that something else is going on beyond mere statements of musical taste, significance or insignificance, and judgments of good and bad. Readings and interpretations of *A Love Supreme* have obviously been influenced by the passage of time but the idealized perception of the suite separates the work from the context of its creation. Hearing Archie Shepp in particular invade this idealized space is as disturbing as it is refreshing, and reminds us of how recordings—like history itself—are constructs that feed our desires, respond to societal needs, and reflect our aspirations. Treating Shepp's playing as a type of historical intervention—a sonic thunderbolt that was sounded in 1964 but only recently heard—the sounds draw our attention to the canonical status of jazz, with its surrounding mythologies and naturalized discourse, which restore a perhaps hitherto silent sense of politics to the listening experience.

3. Contending Forces: *A Love Supreme* and Dialogism

The final example of the ideological framing of *A Love* Supreme shows how values and beliefs bound up with the album can be applied retrospectively, not only providing a means of authenticating African American culture from the mid-1960s to the present day but also influencing our understanding of the world before *A Love Supreme* came into existence. Echoing Amiri Baraka's idea that the values embodied in the music of Coltrane were in existence before a note was sounded, *A Love Supreme* has become an authenticating statement for African American culture in general, regardless of the period in question. Applying the influence of *A Love Supreme* retrospectively conjures up Mikhail Bakhtin's concept of dialogism, in which cultural and historical influence is understood as a two-way channel: the past influences the present, but occurrences in the present can continually change our perceptions of the past.[53] This not only creates retrospective readings of *A Love Supreme* in which we understand Coltrane's life and works as teleologically determined (in other words, all roads lead to *A Love Supreme*) but also encourages us to apply the influence of *A Love Supreme*, more broadly, to the progress of African American history.

A crude example of this process in action can be seen by the way in which Pauline Hopkins's 1900 novel *Contending Forces: A Romance Illustrative of Negro Life North and South* was renamed *A Love Supreme* in 1997. By using *A Love Supreme* as a "new title" Hopkins's novel becomes integrally linked both to Coltrane's seminal work and also, perhaps more important, to the values of African American history. Overarching tropes play out for both literature and music, as the continuity of tradition and essential beliefs of an imagined community are celebrated through Coltrane's famous title. *A Love Supreme* is considered a title that is as ancient as it is modern, and it connotes a set of core values. Although the renaming of Hopkins's novel could be read as a simple marketing stunt, employing a title that will resonate more easily with modern audiences, the use of *A Love Supreme* in this context is clearly ideological, especially when we think about how certain themes within the novel are accentuated over others. Since the 1970s, Hopkins's writing has been rediscovered and celebrated among scholars of African American literature. And yet, some scholars have debated the dominant interpretations of Hopkins's work, questioning the extent to which race and political activism should be used as key components in the author's work.

Jill Bergman, for example, sees the renaming of *Contending Forces* as symptomatic of a wider ideological sea change in African American scholarship:

> These reprints attempt to lift Hopkins out of the post-Reconstruction milieu in which she lived and wrote and set her down in an era of radical race activism reminiscent of the nineteen sixties. They flatten out her complexity and try to fit her into a comfortable pattern of race activism that will, presumably, sell to modern readers. But upon reflection I began to wonder whether her recent scholarly recuperation lends itself to—even calls into being—such a revision of her oeuvre.[54]

Bergman stresses that current readings of Hopkins's life and work tend to foreground racial aspects over gender issues, and ignore historical evidence that clearly problematizes these, now dominant, interpretations of the writer's work. Explaining this tendency, Bergman states that simplified readings are born out of a desire to maintain the myth of Hopkins's political radicalism despite evidence to the contrary. Bergman stresses that these dominant interpretations ultimately stem from scholarly bias; however, the issue is not only about downplaying gender but is also representative of "an ongoing problem of 'one-factor analyses' which oversimplify the complexities of identity and politics."[55] Bergman's critique highlights the way in which *A Love Supreme* has become a shorthand for a particular world view that binds African American culture together, albeit with the reconstituted and idealized values of the 1960s.

When we compare this process to Coltrane, we can observe a number of parallels between the ideological control of both Hopkins and Coltrane. Indeed, Bergman's discussion of critical bias, simplified narratives, and limited representations mirrors the themes that have run through this study. Furthermore, it is important to consider how applying values from the present day and to readings of historical contexts is a dangerous process. These skewed interpretations of the past can be countered with a different type of revisionism, one that advocates complexity, contradiction, and an acknowledgment of the different ideological perspectives at play.

BEYOND *A LOVE SUPREME*

By his own constant example, John himself always implied it's O.K. to go deeper and examine things, to expand one's understanding of the music.[56]

Ravi Coltrane's reading of his father's approach to music seems the perfect way to conclude a study of *A Love Supreme*. In going deeper, and seeking to expand our understanding of music, I argue that we need to move away from established convention, dominant interpretations, and dogma toward an appreciation of complexity, contradiction, and alternate readings of recordings and their place in history. In many respects, approaches to Coltrane scholarship should echo Coltrane's own approach to music: rather than being unified, safe, and predictable, research into Coltrane's music should be provocative, experimental, and multidimensional. As Peter Watrous suggests, talking about the years following Coltrane's death, the widespread appeal of the artist and his approach to musical creation could provide us with a model for change: "[After] decades of often jarring cultural and political cynicism, his trademarks of honesty, forthrightness, and overwhelming desire to change, to do things that haven't been done before, seem more than just appealing. They seem necessary."[57]

I believe that *A Love Supreme* provides us with a vehicle for understanding the possibilities of what recordings can be. By understanding ways in which recordings inspire listeners at the same time as exerting their own cultural influence, we become aware of the potential of recordings and their central place in the construction of jazz history. The examples and observations made throughout this book not only demonstrate how values of the present ultimately have an impact on our perception of the past but also highlight the way in which the cultural influence of recordings moves in different historical directions. By moving beyond *A Love Supreme* we can understand how recordings have the potential to be viewed both as reified objects with dominant or fixed meanings and as fluid cultural signifiers. To understand this complexity, it is clear that we should not always look to the recorded objects themselves for understanding but instead to the conditions and circumstances that brought them into existence in the first place, and their subsequent uses and influences. In adopting this approach, we can open doors to alternative interpretations of music on record and reevaluate the complexity of history itself.

NOTES

PRELIMS

1. Peter Watrous, "John Coltrane: A Life Supreme," in Woideck, C. (ed.), *The John Coltrane Companion* (London and New York: Omnibus Press, 1998), p. 57.

2. Bernard Drayton, quoted in the liner notes to *The Olatunji Concert: The Last Live Recording* [CD reissue] (Verve Music Group, Impulse 314 589 120-2, 2001).

3. Francis Newton [Eric Hobsbawm], *The Jazz Scene* (London: Penguin, 1961), p. 155.

4. Archie Shepp, quoted in Lol Lovett (dir.), *Saint John Coltrane* (2004), broadcast June 16, 2004, as part of the BBC *Imagine* documentary series.

5. Dave Liebman, "John Coltrane," *Jazz Research Journal* 2.2 (2008), p. 111.

INTRODUCTION

1. Jed Rasula, "The Media of Memory: The Seductive Menace of Records in Jazz History," in Gabbard, K. (ed.), *Jazz Among the Discourses* (Durham and London: Duke University Press, 1995), pp. 134–164.

2. Martin Williams, *The Jazz Tradition* (Oxford and New York: Oxford University Press, 1983), p. 251 fn. 2.

3. Michael Jarrett, *Drifting on a Read: Jazz as a Model for Writing* (Albany: State University of New York Press, 1999), p. 184.

4. For a literal example of the political influence of jazz recordings, one can consider the way in which Miles Davis's *Kind of Blue* was cited as an inspiration behind Maurice Glasman's concept of "Blue Labour" in the United Kingdom. Lord Glasman posited the idea in 2009 and then again in April 2011 as a supposed alternative to the "Red Tory." See Suzanne Moore, "I Suspect Blue Labour Is Just Another Great Moving-Right Show," *Guardian*, June 25, 2011, p. 36, http://www.guardian.co.uk/commentisfree/2011/jun/24/suzanne-moore-blue-labour.

5. Guthrie Ramsey, "Who Hears Here? Black Music, Critical Bias, and the Musicological Skin Trade," *Musical Quarterly* 85:1 (Spring 2001), p. 20.

6. See Lewis Porter, *John Coltrane: His Life and Music* (Ann Arbor, MI: University of Michigan Press, 1998).

7. Ashley Kahn, *A Love Supreme: The Creation of John Coltrane's Classic Album* (London: Granta Books, 2002).

8. As an illustration, consider the breadth of the following sample of texts published over the last five years: Leonard Brown's edited volume *John Coltrane & Black America's Quest for Freedom* (New York: Oxford University Press, 2010), which explores Coltrane in the context of spiritual values and a an African American aesthetic; Ben Ratliff's modern biography *Coltrane: The Story of a Sound* (London and New York: Faber and Faber, 2007); David Ake's *Jazz Matters* (Berkeley: University of California Press, 2010), which examines the construction of Coltrane mythologies; Chris DeVito's *Coltrane on Coltrane: The Coltrane Interviews* (Chicago, IL: A Cappella Books, 2010), an updated collection of Coltrane's own words and interviews; or the numerous Coltrane essays published in peer-reviewed journals such as *Jazz Research Journal* 2.2 (November 2008) and 3.1 (May 2009) and *Jazz Perspectives* 1.2 (2007).

9. Dave Liebman, "John Coltrane," *Jazz Research Journal* 2.2 (2008), p. 118.

10. See Michael Maher's BBC report, *Saving the House of Jazz Legend John Coltrane*, January 20, 2012. http://www.bbc.co.uk/news/entertainment-arts-16643652.

CHAPTER 1

1. Krin Gabbard, "The Word 'Jazz,'" in Cook, Mervyn, and Horn, David (eds.), *The Cambridge Companion to Jazz* (Cambridge: Cambridge University Press, 2002), p. 5.

2. Peter Townsend, *Jazz in American Culture* (Edinburgh: Edinburgh University Press, 2000), p. 168.

3. Ibid., p. 168.

4. Leonard Brown, "You Have to Be Invited: Reflections on Music Making and Musician Creation in Black American Culture," in Brown, L. (ed.), *John Coltrane & Black America's Quest for Freedom* (New York: Oxford University Press, 2010), p. 6.

5. Ibid., viii.

6. See, for example, David Ake, *Jazz Cultures* (Berkeley: University of California Press, 2002); E. Taylor Atkins, *Jazz Planet* (Jackson: University of Mississippi Press, 2003); Richard Sudhalter, *Lost Chords: White Musicians and Their Contribution to Jazz* (New York: Oxford University Press, 1999); and Sherrie Tucker, *Swing Shift: "All Girl" Bands of the 1940s* (Durham and London: Duke University Press, 2000).

7. Consider, for example, George Lewis's "Improvised Music Post-1950: Afrological and Eurological Perspectives," *Black Music Research Journal* 16.1 (Spring 1996), pp. 91–122.

8. Lewis Porter, *John Coltrane* (Ann Arbor: University of Michigan Press, 1998), p. 249.

9. I discuss this later in relation to the formal structure of the album.

10. Ashley Kahn, *A Love Supreme*, pp. 97 and 99.

11. Ravi Coltrane, "Divining a Spiritual Center," in the CD booklet of John Coltrane's *A Love Supreme* (Deluxe Edition) [CD reissue] (Impulse Records 2002, catalogue number 589 945–2), p. 22.

12. Ibid., p. 24.

13. Ibid., p. 24.

14. See Coltrane's liner notes to *A Love Supreme*.

15. Even when the term "composition" was used by Coltrane's contemporaries and advocates of the "New Thing," the term was still contested. Consider, for example, the creation of the Jazz Composers Guild in 1964 and the politics surrounding definitions of group ideals and membership. Carla Bley, for example, not only served as a problematic member of the group in terms of race and gender but also created tensions within the group due to her status as a jazz composer and not a jazz performer-composer. See, Benjamin Piekut, "Race, Community, and Conflict in the Jazz Composers Guild," *Jazz Perspectives* 3.3 (December 2009), pp. 191–231.

16. I discuss the impact of historical recordings and the desire for reenactment in my book *Jazz Icons: Heroes, Myths and the Jazz Tradition* (Cambridge: Cambridge University Press, 2010). For examples of how recordings reify performance practices, see Jed Rasula, "The Media of Memory: The Seductive Menace of Records in Jazz History" in Gabbard, K. (ed.), *Jazz Among the Discourses* (Durham and London: Duke University Press, 1995), pp. 134–162; and Robert Walser, "Out of Notes: Signification, Interpretation and the Problem of Miles Davis" *Musical Quarterly* 77.2 (Summer 1993), pp. 343–365. For a discussion of the concept of musical "works," see Lydia Goehr, *The Imaginary Museum of Musical Works: An Essay in the Philosophy of Music* (Oxford and New York: Oxford University Press, 1992).

17. Alice Coltrane quoted in Ashley Kahn, *A Love Supreme*, p. xv.

18. Ben Ratliff, *Coltrane*, p. 90. The *A Love Supreme* manuscript is now housed at the Smithsonian Institution.

19. Coltrane stated this desire in his interview with Kitty Grime. See Kitty Grime, "John Coltrane Talks to Jazz News," reproduced in DeVito, C. (ed.), *Coltrane on Coltrane: The John Coltrane Interviews* (Chicago, IL: A Cappella Books, 2010), pp. 119–121.

20. Barry Kernfeld quoted in Paul Berliner, *Thinking in Jazz* (Chicago: University of Chicago Press, 1994), p. 795 fn. 3.

21. McCoy Tyner quoted in Kahn, *A Love Supreme*, p. 92.

22. Elvin Jones quoted in Kahn, *A Love Supreme*, pp. 92–93.

23. Ibid., p. 93.

24. Rudy van Gelder, quoted in Lol Lovett (dir.), *Saint John Coltrane* (2004), broadcast June 16, 2004, as part of the BBC *Imagine* documentary series.

25. Branford Marsalis interview with Alice Coltrane is featured on Pierre Lamoureux (dir.), *Branford Marsalis Quartet: Coltrane's A Love Supreme Live in Amsterdam* [DVD] (Cambridge, MA: Marsalis Music, 2004).

26. Michael Jarrett, *Drifting on a Read: Jazz as a Model for Writing* (Albany: State University of New York Press, 1999), p. 64.

27. Derrida quoted in John Storey, *Cultural Theory and Popular Culture: An Introduction*, (Harlow, UK: Prentice Hall, 2006), p. 100.

28. Ibid. See also Jacques Derrida, *Positions* (London: Continuum Press, 2010).

29. John Coltrane, liner notes to *A Love Supreme* (Deluxe Edition), p. 26.

30. Ibid., p. 26.

31. John Tchicai in conversation with the author, October 2010.

32. Ben Ratliff, *Coltrane*, p. x.

33. See, for example, Val Wilmer's, *As Serious as Your Life: John Coltrane and Beyond* (London: Serpent's Tail, 1992); or Dave Liebman's "John Coltrane," *Jazz Research Journal* 2.2 (November 2008), pp. 109–118, for firsthand accounts of encounters with Coltrane.

34. See, for example, Mark Katz, *Capturing Sound: How Technology Changed Music* (Berkeley: University of California Press, 2004); Jed Rasula, "The Media of Memory"; and Michael Chanan, *Repeated Takes: A Short History of Recording and Its Effects on Music* (London: Verso, 1995).

35. Evan Eisenberg, *The Recording Angel: Music, Records and Culture from Aristotle to Zappa*, 2nd ed. (New Haven, CT: Yale University Press, 2005), p. 120.

36. Although I would have loved to experience Coltrane's music in a live setting, I am fascinated by the way in which recordings can have an even more profound impact on listeners than live music or audiovisual evidence. As an illustration of the power of records through time, one has to think only about Sonny Rollins and the way in which his current music is considered different, not just when compared with Coltrane (his contemporary) today but also in relation to his own seminal works of the 1950s.

37. This is obviously not an unusual occurrence as most live performances display an element of flexibility with time when compared to their studio equivalents.

38. Ashley Kahn, liner notes to *A Love Supreme* (Deluxe Edition).

39. See Michiel De Ruyter, "Interview with John Coltrane" reproduced in DeVito, C. (ed.), *Coltrane on Coltrane: The John Coltrane Interviews* (Chicago, IL: A Cappella Books, 2010), p. 252.

40. Jed Rasula, "The Media of Memory." See also my discussion of jazz photography in *Jazz Icons* (2010).

41. For more details of the Antibes concert, see Kahn, *A Love Supreme*, pp. 167–173.

42. Katz, *Capturing Sound*, pp. 3–7.

43. John Corbett, *Extended Play: Sounding Off from John Cage to Dr. Funkenstein* (Durham and London: Duke University Press, 1994).

44. Ibid., p. 41.

45. As an example of a way in which recordings encourage a detachment from time and space, consider Will Straw's study of gender and recordings. Straw describes how, historically, recordings became objects of private havens, providing men with fetish objects that had a sensual/sexual quality and social function. Although Straw suggests that there is nothing intrinsic in the collecting of records that would lead them to become associated with the construction of masculinity, records participate in the gendering of cultural habits. The salvaging of cultural artifacts leads to the stereotypical view of the domestic spaces of men. On the one hand, there is the portrayal of the slovenly bachelor pad with records sprawled across it, and on the other the depiction of men as obsessively ordered and systematic in their archiving of personal objects. It is

through the relationship to collection that a man's ideas about domestic stability or organization of his domestic environment come to fruition; take, for example, the ideal of the 1950s listening room with the hi-fi taking center stage. This environment was felt to nourish a masculine ideal as a refuge from the noise and interruption of everyday married and family life. Recordings in this context are treated as an escape from domesticity and social responsibility. See Will Straw, "Sizing Up Record Collections: Gender and Connoisseurship in Rock Music Culture," in Whiteley, Sheila (ed.), *Sexing the Groove: Popular Music and Gender* (New York: Routledge, 1997), pp. 3–16.

46. I develop this idea in T. Whyton, "Four for Trane: Jazz and the Disembodied Voice," *Jazz Perspectives* 1.2 (October 2007), pp. 115–132.

47. Neil Leonard, *Jazz: Myth and Religion* (New York and Oxford: Oxford University Press, 1987).

CHAPTER 2

1. Martin Williams, *The Jazz Tradition*, p. 255–256.

2. Musician Don Pate paraphrased in Paul Berliner, *Thinking in Jazz: The Infinite Art of Improvisation* (Chicago and London: University of Chicago Press, 1994), p. 30.

3. Charles Tolliver quoted in Ben Ratliff, *Coltrane: The Story of a Sound* (London and New York: Faber and Faber, 2007), p. 149.

4. See, for example, Krin Gabbard, "The Jazz Canon and Its Consequences," in Gabbard, *Jazz Among the Discourses*, pp. 1–28; Scott Deveaux, "Constructing the Jazz Tradition: Jazz Historiography," *Black American Literature Forum* 25:3 (Autumn 1991), pp. 525–560; and John Gennari, "Jazz Criticism: Its Development and Ideologies," *Black American Literature Forum* 25:3 (Fall 1991), pp. 449–523.

5. See Sherrie Tucker, *Swing Shift: "All Girl" Bands of the 1940s* (Durham and London: Duke University Press, 2000); and Nichole T. Rustin (ed.), *Big Ears: Listening for Gender in Jazz Studies* (Durham and London: Duke University Press, 2008).

6. See Wynton Marsalis with Geoffrey C. Ward, *Moving to Higher Ground: How Jazz Can Change Your Life* (New York: Random House, 2008).

7. See DeVeaux, "Constructing the Jazz Tradition," p. 525.

8. Ekkehard Jost, *Free Jazz* (New York: Da Capo Press, 1994), pp. 32–33.

9. Ratliff, *Coltrane*, p. 90.

10. I discuss this point in more detail in my *Jazz Icons* (2010). For example, the way in which Ellington's sacred works fulfill this role or the mystery surrounding unfinished works such as Mozart's *Requiem* or Bach's *Art of Fugue*; the romantic ideal promotes the last work as the most sacred.

11. I discuss this in more detail in chapter 3.

12. This change in perception works well in relation to Coltrane as the artist died in 1967, a relatively short time following the production of *A Love Supreme*. The change in persona for artists can also work in other ways: for example, consider the way in which the work of Sonny Rollins of the 1950s is separated in from his current music or how Paul McCartney is perceived today in relation

to his time as a member of the Beatles. Representation serves to distance living figures from the mysterious and iconic performances of the past.

13. See David Ake, *Jazz Matters* (Berkeley: University of California Press, 2010).

14. For examples of musicians' accounts of Coltrane's transcendent and God-like qualities, see Berliner, *Thinking in Jazz*, p. 32; and Graham Lock, "Trane Talk," *Wire* 86 (April 1991), pp. 42–43.

15. Even though subsequent albums such as *Meditations* adhered to similar principles, *A Love Supreme* had been presented as the embodiment of these core values. In mythic representations of Coltrane, moving beyond *A Love Supreme* required a different set of narrative devices to describe and analyze music even where it shared similarities with *A Love Supreme*.

16. Jost, *Free Jazz*, p. 32.

17. See Frank Kofsky, *John Coltrane and the Jazz Revolution of the 1960s* (London and New York: Pathfinder Press, 1998), p. 130. Although skewed by a Marxist agenda and a deep-rooted, and at times essentialist, promotion of black nationalist ideals, Kofsky's writings serve to highlight the relationship between artistic production and the broader social and political context in which music is created. In seeking to examine the potential for ideological interest in music, Kofsky provides a means of questioning the dominant social order and the official histories of jazz as promoted through the majority of writings on the subject. Kofsky's mourning the loss of Coltrane as an avant-garde leader, for example, encourages us to imagine how Coltrane and *A Love Supreme* would be perceived today had Coltrane's career as an experimental avant-gardist extended to the present day.

18. For Ravi Coltrane's comments on the sacred quality of *A Love Supreme* see Kahn, *A Love Supreme*, p. 206.

19. See, for example, Porter, *John Coltrane*, p. 196; and Ratliff, *Coltrane*, p. 79.

20. For example, see Kofsky, *John Coltrane*, p. 302. Bob Thiele's account of this period is slightly different as he suggested that the projects came out "because of the jazz critics." Even though Thiele acknowledged the fact that the *Ballads* album was his suggestion, he portrayed the partnership between himself and Coltrane as one of consensus: "Both as a musical document and personal statement, John loved recording that album, and immediately became anxious to do a follow-up." Bob Thiele (with Bob Golden), *What a Wonderful World: A Lifetime of Recordings* (New York and Oxford: Oxford University Press, 1995), pp. 123–124.

21. See Ratliff, *Coltrane*, pp. 79–82.

22. Ashley Kahn, *A Love Supreme*, pp. 216–217.

23. Ratliff suggests that Coltrane was not thinking about career progression (and by implication, thus commercial success) by following *My Favorite Things* with collaborations with Dolphy, reinforcing the idea that he was not concerned with cultivating his audience or managing the ways in which he was represented. Equally, he uses Coltrane's shift from Dolphy to his *Ballads* album as evidence of the artist not being political, posing the question of why a politically active musician would choose to undertake a range of conformist album projects. See Ratliff, *Coltrane*, p. 79. Although this is one interpretation

of events, the move from more commercially oriented projects to more experimental outputs does not necessarily have to be viewed in this way. Indeed,
Coltrane's negotiation of different performance projects paves the way for
future jazz artists who walk the line between commercial and experimental
pursuits (one only needs to think of the work of the output of Pat Metheny, for
example, to witness an artist navigating different contexts within the recording
industry). In contrast to Ratliff's argument, these examples could easily demonstrate Coltrane's awareness of market forces, and the need to remain in the
public eye and to appeal to different audiences.

24. Porter, *John Coltrane*, pp. 190–191. See also Lorenzo Thomas, "Ascension:
Music and the Black Arts Movement," in Gabbard, K. (ed.), *Jazz Among the
Discourses*, pp. 256–274, for a discussion of Coltrane's influence at Impulse!
Records and an evaluation of Coltrane's political activities.

25. For more information on the history and development of Impulse! Records,
see Ashley Kahn, *The House That Trane Built: The Story of Impulse Records*
(London: Granta Books, 2006).

26. Consider, for example, Impulse cover designs and titles for albums including
Oliver Nelson's *Blues and the Abstract Truth,* Archie Shepp's *Fire Music,* or
Charles Mingus's *Black Saint and the Sinner Lady.*

27. Impulse did move away from the orange and black spine on later occasions.
Coltrane's *Africa Brass Sessions, Vol. 2,* for example, released in 1974, did not
include the distinctive spine.

28. Consider, for example, the way in which Blue Note covers would break the
symmetry of an image with a out-of-place photograph or place text in opposite
directions in order to convey a sense of difference, hipness, or a quirkiness, a
music that was slightly off center. See the cover to Freddie Hubbard's 1962
album *Hub-Tones* for an example of broken symmetry.

29. See Whyton, *Jazz Icons*, pp. 7–8.

30. Michael Jarrett, *Drifting on a Read*, p. 199.

31. For a detailed analysis of Coltrane's poem, see James C Hall, *Mercy, Mercy Me:
African-American Culture and the American Sixties* (New York: Oxford
University Press, 2001).

32. For an interesting parallel discussion of the constructed nature of celebrities,
see Richard Dyer's *Stars* (London: BFI, 1998), and *Heavenly Bodies: Film Stars
and Society* (Hampshire, UK: Palgrave Macmillan, 1987).

33. The notion that music is all that mattered is a common trope in the representation of authentic artists across different genres. In Coltrane's case, the artist's
total immersion in music results in personal anecdotes always relating to the
music in some way. In other words, the biography of Coltrane is always shifted
away from overly personal accounts toward explanations of "the music itself."
This is due to the fact that personal information is either unknown or deemed
to be irrelevant to the wider context of Coltrane mythmaking. This includes a
lack of engagement with Coltrane's private life, from his marriage breakdown
and sexual relationships to drug use to more subtle forms of narrative that promote the music above all else. Ben Ratliff states, "Coltrane had left his wife,
Naima, in the summer of 1963, and shortly thereafter was living with Alice

McLeod, a pianist from Detroit who played bebop and had studied informally with Bud Powell in Paris." Ratliff, *Coltrane*, p. 89. This sentence is quite telling. Not only does Ratliff brush over the complexities and emotional aspects of the marriage breakup but his description of Alice McLeod foregrounds her musical pedigree—this is atypical when compared to the usual gendered description of jazz artists. Usually for example, you would read descriptions such as "lady doctor" or "female composer," or "male nurse," illustrating the way in which gender is typically foregrounded when journalists describe non-normative roles as if, for example, to demonstrate that being a woman is more essential than the jobs women perform. These gendered and often derogatory remarks are often leveled at the spouses of great men. One needs only to think about the way in which Yoko Ono (or more recently, Heather Mills McCartney) was demonized to witness this. Here, on the contrary, McLeod is accepted as a musician *first* and wife second. However, we should take this not necessarily as a powerful example of feminist writing but as a strategy designed to simplify and purify the Coltrane discourse; even in marriage, relationships are secondary to the "music itself."

34. P. Auslander, *Liveness: Performance in a Mediatized Culture* (London and New York: Routledge, 1999), p. 3.

35. Ibid., p. 10. For writings on the interplay between jazz recordings and performance, see Jed Rasula, "The Media of Memory"; and Mark Katz, *Capturing Sound: How Technology Changed Music* (Berkeley: University of California Press, 2004).

36. Jack Cooke, "Chasin' the Trane," *Wire* 86 (April 1991), p. 32.

37. Ashley Kahn, *A Love Supreme*, p. xix.

38. Shoichi Yui, Kiyoshi Koyama, Kazuaki Tsujimoto, et al., "Interviews with John Coltrane" reproduced in DeVito, C. (ed.), *Coltrane on Coltrane: The John Coltrane Interviews* (Chicago, IL: A Cappella Books, 2010), p. 270.

39. Martin Smith, *John Coltrane: Jazz, Racism and Resistance* (London: Redwords, 2006), p. 83.

40. Woideck, *The John Coltrane Companion*, p. 35.

41. Quoted in Val Wilmer, *As Serious as Your Life* (London: Serpent's Tail, 1992), p. 44.

42. Quoted in Kahn, *A Love Supreme*, p. 197.

43. Quoted in Lock, "Trane Talk," *Wire* 86 (April 1991), p. 43.

44. For examples of the comparisons between Charlie Parker and religious figures, see Jon Panish, *The Color of Jazz: Race and Representation in Postwar American Culture* (Jackson: University of Mississippi Press, 1997).

45. Quoted in Lock, "Trane Talk," p. 43.

46. Paul Berliner, *Thinking in Jazz: The Infinite Art of Improvisation* (Chicago and London: University of Chicago Press, 1994), p. 32.

47. For example, Berliner offers accounts of musical transfiguration where listeners are affected deeply by music in their subconscious. He states, "After John Coltrane's death, a musician was once awakened by a vivid dream in which Coltrane's group presented a sensational and extraordinarily vibrant performance, one that the musician could not recall ever having heard before.

He struggled to recall fragments of its sounds as they receded from his memory. Although the experience left him but a small legacy of actual music, the psychological and emotional impressions were lasting ones." Berliner, *Thinking in Jazz*, p. 142. Although imagined, this provides an example of the power and influence of Coltrane's music on listeners.

48. Quoted in Barry Witherden, "Blowin' into History" *Wire* 86 (April 1991), p. 41.

49. Neil Leonard, *Jazz: Myth and Religion* (New York: Oxford University Press, 1987), p. 42. See also Emile Durkheim [trans. Carol Cosman], *The Elementary Forms of Religious Life* (New York: Oxford University Press World Classics, 2008); and Max Weber, *The Protestant Ethic and the Spirit of Capitalism* (New York: Dover, 2003 [1958]).

50. C. O. Simpkins, *Coltrane: A Biography* (Perth Amboy, NJ: Herndon House, 1975), p. 60.

51. See, for example, Leonard L. Brown, "In His Own Words: Coltrane's Responses to Critics," in Brown, L. L. (ed.), *John Coltrane & Black America's Quest for Freedom*, pp. 15–17.

52. Porter, *John Coltrane*, p. 44.

53. Bill Cole, *John Coltrane* (New York: Da Capo Press, 2001), p. 23.

54. Ibid., p. 87.

55. See Bertrand Lauer, "John Coltrane and the Replacement Child Syndrome," *Jazz Research Journal* 3.1 (2009), pp. 105–117.

56. David Ake, *Jazz Cultures* (Berkeley: University of California Press, 2002), p. 128.

57. Saint John Coltrane African Orthodox Church website, http://www.coltranechurch.org/#!about2/c4nz [accessed July 6, 2011].

58. Philip Watson, "Out of This World," *Wire* 86 (April 1991), p. 34.

CHAPTER 3

1. Scott Saul, *Freedom Is, Freedom Ain't: Jazz and the Making of the Sixties* (Cambridge MA and London: Harvard University Press, 2003), pp. 8–9.

2. Lewis Porter, *John Coltrane*, p. 262.

3. Philip Larkin, "All What Jazz?" reproduced in Gottlieb, R. (ed.), *Reading Jazz: A Gathering of Autobiography, Reportage and Criticism from 1919 to Now* (London: Bloomsbury, 1997), pp. 803–804.

4. David Ake, *Jazz Cultures*, pp. 129–145.

5. Ake, *Jazz Cultures*, p. 145.

6. Martin Williams, *The Jazz Tradition* (Oxford and New York: Oxford University Press, 1983), pp. 233–234.

7. Williams's *The Jazz Tradition* pays homage to F. R. Leavis's work *The Great Tradition* (London: Faber and Faber, 2008) in its canon building and its celebration of all that is great and good about a civilization. Leavis also promoted the belief that culture should remain in "minority keeping" and expressed a genuine fear of the subversive qualities of mass culture. These characteristics can also be read into Williams's mission, constructing a view of jazz that is both elitist and detached from popular culture. For further reading on the Williams's

work as ideology, see Scott DeVeaux, "Core and Boundaries," *The Source* 2 (March 2005), pp. 15–30; and John Gennari, *Blowin' Hot and Cool: Jazz and Its Critics* (Chicago and London: University of Chicago Press, 2006).

8. Williams, *The Jazz Tradition*, pp. 231–232.

9. Amiri Baraka, "Jazz and the White Critic," in Jones, L. [Amiri Baraka], *Black Music* (New York: Da Capo Press, 1998 [1968]), p. 19.

10. Lorenzo Thomas, "Ascension: Music and the Black Arts Movement," in Gabbard, K. (ed.), *Jazz Among the Discourses*, pp. 256–274.

11. See Eric Nisenson, *Ascension: John Coltrane and His Quest* (New York: Da Capo Press, 1995), p. 222.

12. Ratliff, *Coltrane*, p. 199.

13. Stanley Crouch, *Considering Genius* (New York: Basic Civitas Books, 2006), p. 214.

14. For a selection of writings on the blues aesthetic and African American hero figure, see Albert Murray's books, *From the Briarpatch File: On Context, Procedure and American Identity* (New York: Pantheon Books, 2001); *Stomping the Blues* (London: Quartet Books, 1978); and *The Omni-Americans: New Perspectives on Black Experience and American Culture* (New York: Outerbridge & Dienstfrey, 1970).

15. Porter, *John Coltrane*, p. 265.

16. Shepp quoted in A. B. Spellman's liner notes to the album. See *Ascension* [CD Reissue] (Verve Music Group, Impulse Records AS-95, 2009).

17. Ekkehard Jost, *Free Jazz* (New York: Da Capo Press, 1994), p. 89.

18. See Porter, *Coltrane*, p. 72.

19. See, for example, George E. Lewis, *A Power Stronger Than Itself: The AACM and American Experimental Music* (Chicago and London: University of Chicago Press, 2008); Benjamin Piekut, "Race, Community, and Conflict in the Jazz Composers Guild"; and Glenn Gould, "The Prospects of Recording" in Page, T., *The Glenn Gould Reader* (London: Faber and Faber, 1987), pp. 331–353.

20. Ratliff, *Coltrane*, p. 97.

21. See Ratliff, *Coltrane*, pp. 97–99. The statement that *Ascension* "had to happen" draws parallels to narratives associated with Schoenberg's expressionism and the move into atonality. On Coltrane's performance practice and last years, Ratliff borrows a quote from Rashied Ali, saying that Coltrane's chanting, beating of the chest, and so on was a result of having played everything on his horn. This quotation mirrors the modernist romance of expressionism where Coltrane (as did Schoenberg) sought a means of expression in whatever form, even when language, or his normal musical outlets, could no longer suffice. See Ratliff, *Coltrane*, p. 109. For a version of the Schoenberg inevitability narrative, see Paul Griffiths, *Modern Music: A Concise History from Debussy to Boulez* (New York: Thames and Hudson, 1990), pp. 28–34.

22. Ratliff, *Coltrane*, p. 155.

23. Lewis Porter, *John Coltrane*, p. 266.

24. A. B. Spellman, liner notes to *Ascension*.

25. Tolliver quoted in Ratliff, *Coltrane*, p. 153–154. Ratliff states that "this time his audience were even less forgiving, and as a result he undermined his own credibility. Most of his fans could go with his new music as long as band members of repute were playing it. With new members with less objectively measurable talent, some felt they were being conned." Ibid., p. 95.

26. David G. Such, *Avant-Garde Jazz Musicians: Performing "Out There"* (Iowa City: University of Iowa Press, 1993), p. 10.

27. Quoted in Arthur Taylor, *Notes and Tones: Musician-to-Musician Interviews*, 2nd ed. (New York: Da Capo Press, 1993), p. 46.

28. For more on this, see Porter, *John Coltrane*, pp. 266–268.

29. Doug Ramsey quoted in Francis Davis "Take the Coltrane," *Village Voice* (February 18, 1992), reprinted in Woideck, C. (ed.), *The John Coltrane Companion: Five Decades of Commentary* (London: Omnibus Press, 1998), pp. 78–79.

30. The noncanonical model of music making has a parallel to the development of community music, or music that is established beyond the confines of formal music making. Although communal practices have a valuable role to play socially, they are often portrayed as antithetical to the dominant aesthetics of Western art music. For an overview of the politics of Western art music, see Christopher Small, *Musicking; The Meanings of Performing and Listening* (Middletown, CT: Wesleyan University Press, 1998).

31. Ibid., p. 2.

32. Hall, *Mercy Mercy Me*, p. 139.

33. Ibid., p. 142.

34. John Gennari, *Blowin' Hot and Cool*, p. 255.

35. For a contextual overview of the period, see Thomas, "Ascension: Music and the Black Arts Movement"; and Piekut, "Race, Community, and Conflict in the Jazz Composers Guild."

36. Porter, *Coltrane*, p. 277.

37. For a detailed analysis of this technique and other improvisatory devices, see Porter's analysis of Coltrane's "Venus" from *Interstellar Space*. Porter, *Coltrane*, pp. 280–88.

38. Ratliff, *Coltrane*, p. 171.

39. Francis Davis, liner notes to *Interstellar Space* [CD reissue] (Verve Music Group, Impulse Records 543 415–2, 2000).

40. James Hall, *Mercy, Mercy, Me*, p. 23.

41. Ronald Radano, *Lying Up a Nation: Race and Black Music* (Chicago and London: University of Chicago Press, 2003), p. 35.

42. Hall, *Mercy, Mercy, Me*, p. 34.

43. Saul, *Freedom Is, Freedom Ain't*, p. 248.

44. Leonard Brown's "you have to be invited" sums up the essentialist claims to exclusive ownership found within writings on Coltrane.

45. Radano, *Lying Up a Nation*, pp. 35–36.

46. Ratliff, *Coltrane*, p. 174.

47. There had been discussions about Coltrane setting up a recording label, but it is unclear whether the Olatunji Concert would have formed part of these plans.

48. Porter notes that recordings such as Coltrane's *Expression* were drawn from four recording sessions of Spring 1967, but the dating of this material on the record sleeve is inconsistent with the studio logs.

49. Leroi Jones [Amiri Baraka], *Black Music*, p. 176.

50. Baraka quoted in Saul, *Freedom Is, Freedom Ain't*, p. 229.

51. This point is taken up by Saul who claims that "Coltrane was an avatar of black vernacular modernism, a hero who confronted older forms in order to dispose of them—and, in the process, made himself unrecognizable to his previous selves." See Saul, *Freedom Is, Freedom Ain't*, p. 229.

52. Tommy Lott, "When Bar Walkers Preach: John Coltrane and the Crisis of the Black Intellectual," in Brown, L. (ed.), *John Coltrane & Black America's Quest for Freedom* (New York: Oxford University Press, 2010), pp. 102, 105.

53. Ratliff, *Coltrane*, p. 174.

54. Radano discusses this issue in his book *Lying Up a Nation*. Interestingly, Radano describes the way in which constructions of essential blackness have been negotiated but appear naturalized, appealing to different communities of interest. "Because we have continued to believe that racial differences are real, however, we as a nation and as an interracial people have repeatedly sought to enact those differences in sound, just as African American musicians in particular have been motivated and rewarded both socially and economically for realizing versions of black musical distinctiveness," p. xiii.

55. Dave Liebman, "John Coltrane," *Jazz Research Journal* 2.2 (2008), p. 115.

56. Frank Kofsky, "Interview with John Coltrane," reprinted in Chris DeVito, *Coltrane on Coltrane: The John Coltrane Interviews* (Chicago, IL: A Cappella Books, 2010), p. 295.

57. Nat Hentoff, "John Coltrane," *Jazz Is* (1976), reprinted in Woideck, C. (ed.), *The John Coltrane Companion*, p. 52.

CHPATER 4

1. Ashley Kahn, *A Love Supreme*, p. 199.

2. Radano, *Lying Up a Nation*, p. xi.

3. Bill Shoemaker, "Cleaning the Mirror," *Downbeat* (July 1992), p. 27.

4. Bruce Tucker, "Prejudice Lives: Toward a Philosophy of Black Music Biography," *Black Music Research Journal* 4 (1984), pp. 11–12.

5. Ashley Kahn, *A Love Supreme*, p. 203.

6. See, for example, *A Reggae Interpretation of Kind of Blue* (Consart Records 1699088, 2010), or *Kind of Bloop: An 8-Bit Tribute to Miles Davis' Kind of Blue* (www.kindofbloop.com).

7. Kahn, *A Love Supreme*, p. 204.

8. Foster quoted in Kahn, *A Love Supreme*, p. 205.

9. Ravi Coltrane quoted in Kahn, *A Love Supreme*, p. 206.

10. Ibid., p. 208.

11. Liner notes to *Footsteps of Our Fathers* [CD] (Marsalis Music MARCD3301, 2002).

12. Kimberly Benston, *Performing Blackness: Enactments of African-American Modernism* (London and New York: Routledge, 2000), p. 146.

13. Sonia Sanchez, *a/coltrane/poem* (1970), reproduced in Kimberly Benston, *Performing Blackness*, pp. 321–323.

14. Benston, *Performing Blackness*, p. 157.

15. Bruce Tucker, "Toward a Philosophy of Black Music Biography," *Black Music Research Journal* 4 (1984), pp. 11–12.

16. See, for example, Michael S. Harper, "Don't They Speak Jazz," *MELUS* 10.1 [Ethnic Literature and Music] (Spring 1983), pp. 3–6; and Joseph A. Brown, "Their Long Scars Touch Ours: A Reflection on the Poetry of Michael Harper," *Callaloo* 26 (Winter 1986), pp. 209–220.

17. For a close reading of the poem, see Benston, *Performing Blackness*, pp. 177–184.

18. Benston, *Performing Blackness*, p. 181.

19. For more on Harper's influences, see Reginald Martin "An Interview with Michael Harper," *Black American Literature Forum* 24.3 (Autumn 1990), pp. 441–451.

20. Michael Harper quoted in Weatherly, T., and Wilentz, T. (eds.), *Natural Process: An Anthology of New Black Poetry* (New York: Hill and Wang, 1970), p. 43.

21. Michael S. Harper and Paul Austerlitz, *Double Take Jazz-Poetry Conversations* [CD] (INNOVA, 2004).

22. Lars Eckstein, "A Love Supreme: Jazzthetic Strategies in Toni Morrison's *Beloved*," *African American Review* 40.2 (June 2006), p. 273.

23. Ibid., p. 279.

24. Ibid., p. 280.

25. Paul Gilroy's groundbreaking perspectives on diasporic cultures and the resistance to essential black subject positions have also been criticized for their limited discussion of music as a discursive cultural practice. Ronald Radano argues that despite Gilroy's admirable desire to create a music-centered approach to cultural studies, his work falls short in achieving its goals by continuing to treat music as existing by a separate set of rules: "Despite the diversity Gilroy claims for the musics of the 'Black Atlantic,' he remains committed to the politics of center, to a transcendent, purely musical force, that 'gets beyond' the instabilities of discursive contest." Ronald Radano, *Lying Up a Nation*, p. 40.

26. Gareth Griffiths, "The Myth of Authenticity," in Ashcroft, B., Griffiths, G., and Tiffin, H. (eds.), *The Postcolonial Studies Reader* (New York: Routledge, 1999), p. 237.

27. Peter Watrous, "John Coltrane: A Life Supreme," *Musician* (July 1987), reprinted in Woideck, C., *The John Coltrane Companion*, p. 57.

28. Janet Wolff, *The Social Production of Art* (London: Macmillan, 1993), p. 49.

29. Frank Kofsky, *John Coltrane and the Jazz Revolution of the 1960s* (New York: Pathfinder Press, 1998), pp. 433–439.

30. Ravi Coltrane, "Divining a Spiritual Center" in the liner notes to *A Love Supreme* (Deluxe Edition), (2002), p. 24.

31. Ratliff, *Coltrane*, p. xviii.

32. See, for example, Michael Jarrett, *Drifting on a Read*, and my own *Jazz Icons*.

33. Michael Jarrett, *Drifting on a Read*, p. 200.

34. Ellington's *Three Sacred Concerts*, for example, provide an interesting example of the success of spiritually inspired jazz works and tie into the growing interest in spirituality among jazz artists as well as supporting an emerging sense of jazz tradition. Within the traditional domains of contemporary art music composition, religious themes were also being explored at this time. For example, Stravinsky's works such as *Abraham and Isaac* and *Requiem Canticles* or the composer's made-for-TV opera *The Flood*, which was sponsored by a shampoo company, serve as explicit religious works and biblical allegories. Within this context, the growth in religious texts, and search for new outlets for music (cathedrals, concert halls) and modes of expression seemed appropriate for the period.

35. See, for example, La Monte Young's interview as part of the documentary *The World According to John Coltrane* [DVD], directed by Robert Palmer (New York: BMG, 1991).

36. See Andrew Ford, *Composer to Composer: Conversations About Contemporary Music* (London: Quartet Books, 1993), p. 63.

37. Paolo Parisi, *Coltrane* (London: Jonathan Cape, 2012), p. 120.

38. See http://www.supremenewyork.com/random/a_love_supreme [accessed January 3, 2012].

39. For more on the disembodied nature of Coltrane's sound, see my article, "Four for Trane: Jazz and the Disembodied Voice," *Jazz Perspectives* 1.2 (2007), pp. 115–132.

40. For an example of this performance, see http://www.youtube.com/watch?v=83iI53AYTAI [accessed February 19, 2012].

41. See, for example, Norman C. Weinstein, *A Night in Tunisia: Imaginings of Africa in Jazz* (London: Scarecrow Press, 1992); and Ingrid Monson (ed.), *The African Diaspora: A Musical Perspective* (New York and London: Routledge, 2000).

42. Randy Weston quoted in Arthur Taylor (ed.), *Notes and Tones: Musician to Musician Interviews* (New York: Da Capo Press, 1993), p. 30. See also Randy Weston and Willard Jenkins, *African Rhythms: The Autobiography of Randy Weston* (Durham, NC: Duke University Press, 2010).

43. See Frank Kofsky, "Interview with John Coltrane," reproduced in Chris DeVito (ed.), *Coltrane on Coltrane*, p. 291.

44. Steven Feld, *Jazz Cosmopolitanism in Accra: Five Musical Years in Ghana* (Durham, NC, and London: Duke University Press, 2012), p. 24.

45. Wynton Marsalis quoted on the liner notes to *Lincoln Center Jazz Orchestra with Wynton Marsalis: A Love Supreme* [CD] (Palmetto Records PM2106, 2004).

46. See some of the writings on Coltrane that examine synergies and influences from around the world: for example, Hafez Modirzadeh, "Aural Archetypes and Cyclic Perspectives in the Work of John Coltrane and Ancient Chinese Music Theory," *Black Music Research Journal* 21.1 (Spring 2001), pp. 75–106; Carl Clements, "John Coltrane and the Integration of Indian Concepts of Jazz Improvisation," *Jazz Research Journal* 2.2 (November 2008), pp. 155–175;

E. Taylor Atkins, "Sacred Swing: The Sacralization of Jazz in the American Bahá'í Community," *American Music* 24.4 (Winter 2006), pp. 383–420; and Emmanuel Parent and Gregoire Tosser, "The Dilemmas of African-American Orientalism: Coltrane and the Hispanic Imaginary in 'Ole,'" *Jazz Research Journal* 3.1 (May 2009), pp. 63–85.

47. Marsalis feeds directly into the authenticity trope: "The spiritual content of that music is very high, as is the level of seriousness. The conception is a really serious call-and-response conception of playing which is very difficult to understand. Also, harmonically, nobody really knows what Trane was playing.... So a lot of times when you are listening to tunes like those on *A Love Supreme*, that music is so personal and so much Coltrane, so many hours of work and seriousness went into it that it's not something that you're just going to understand overnight.... Coltrane went back to the beginning, and his music really illuminates certain fundamental Afro-American and American conceptions. You have to have an understanding of history to understand his music." See Lolis Eric Elie, "An Interview with Wynton Marsalis," *Callaloo* 13.2 (Spring 1990), pp. 272–273.

48. See the liner notes to *Lincoln Center Jazz Orchestra with Wynton Marsalis: A Love Supreme* [CD] (Palmetto Records PM2106, 2004).

49. Wynton Marsalis and Geoffrey C. Ward, *Moving to Higher Ground: How Jazz Can Change Your Life* (New York: Random House, 2008). This work confirms the heroic ideals of jazz, setting out to demonstrate how great musicians command respect and trust and enrich people's lives.

50. Kahn, *A Love Supreme*, pp. 137–138.

51. Kahn, for example, states that only Shepp and Davis remember the December 10 sessions with any clarity and offers a statement from Elvin Jones in which he claims, "You know, it's a funny thing about it, I know Archie Shepp was there, but I don't remember anything that he did [laughs]. It just didn't register with me." Kahn, *A Love Supreme*, p. 130.

52. Coltrane said, "Well the first part of it, uh, we—Archie Shepp played on it, and I think I had another bass on there, but ah—I didn't use this, this part. Because I had, I had two parts, I had one part that I was singing on, and I had another part—well not singing, chanting—then I had another part that Archie and the other bass was on. And when I—in editing, editing and I, I felt that I wanted to use the part that I had the, uh, the singing on, see. So that's the one we did use." See Michiel de Ruyter, "Interview with John Coltrane" in DeVito, C. (ed.), *Coltrane on Coltrane: The John Coltrane Interviews* (Chicago, IL: A Cappella Books, 2010), p. 249.

53. See Pam Morris (ed.), *The Bakhtin Reader: Selected Writings of Bakhtin, Medvedev and Voloshinov* (London: Edward Arnold, 1994).

54. Jill Bergman, "'Everything We Hoped She'd Be': Contending Forces in Hopkins Scholarship," *African American Review* 38.2 (Summer 2004), p. 182.

55. Ibid., p. 195.

56. Ravi Coltrane, "Divining a Spiritual Center," in the liner notes to John Coltrane's *A Love Supreme* (Deluxe Edition), 2002, p. 22.

57. Peter Watrous, "John Coltrane: A Life Supreme," p. 57.

BIBLIOGRAPHY

Ake, D., *Jazz Cultures*, Berkeley: University of California Press, 2002.

Ake, D., *Jazz Matters*, Berkeley: University of California Press, 2010.

Ake, D., "Learning Jazz, Teaching Jazz," in Cooke, M., and Horn, D. (eds.), *The Cambridge Companion to Jazz*, Cambridge: Cambridge University Press, 2002, 255–269.

Atkins, E. T., *Jazz Planet*, Jackson: University of Mississippi Press, 2003.

Atkins, E. T., "Sacred Swing: The Sacralization of Jazz in the American Bahá'í Community," *American Music*, 24.4 (Winter 2006), 383–420.

Attali, J., *Noise: The Political Economy of Music*, Minneapolis: University of Minnesota Press, 1985.

Auslander, P., *Liveness: Performance in a Mediatized Culture*, London and New York: Routledge, 1999.

Benston, K. W., *Performing Blackness: Enactments of African-American Modernism*, London and New York: Routledge, 2000.

Benston, K. W., and Baraka, A., "Amiri Baraka: An Interview," *Boundary 2* 6.2 (Winter 1978), 303–318.

Bergman, J., "'Everything We Hoped She'd Be': Contending Forces in Hopkins Scholarship," *African American Review* 38.2 (Summer 2004), 181–199.

Berliner, P., *Thinking in Jazz: The Infinite Art of Improvisation*, Chicago and London, University of Chicago Press, 1994.

Boorman, S., "The Musical Text," in Cook, N., and Everist, M. (eds.), *Rethinking Music*, Oxford and New York: Oxford University Press, 2001, 403–442.

Brown, J. A., "Their Long Scars Touch Ours: A Reflection on the Poetry of Michael Harper" *Callaloo* 26 (Winter 1986), 209–220.

Brown, L. (ed.), *John Coltrane & Black America's Quest for Freedom*, New York: Oxford University Press, 2010.

Chanan, M., *Repeated Takes: A Short History of Recording and Its Effects on Music*, London: Verso, 1995.

Clements, C., "John Coltrane and the Integration of Indian Concepts of Jazz Improvisation," *Jazz Research Journal* 2.2 (November 2008), 155–175.

Cole, B., *John Coltrane*, 2nd ed., New York: Da Capo Press, 2001.

Collier, J. L., *The Making of Jazz: A Comprehensive History*, London: Papermac, 1981.

Cooke, J., "Chasin' the Trane," *Wire* 86 (April 1991), 32–33.

Cooke, M., and Horn, D. (eds.), *The Cambridge Companion to Jazz*, Cambridge: Cambridge University Press, 2002.

Corbett, J., *Extended Play: Sounding Off from John Cage to Dr. Funkenstein*, Durham and London: Duke University Press, 1994.

Crouch, S., *Considering Genius: Writings on Music*, New York: Basic Civitas Books, 2006.

Cuscuna, M., "'Strictly on the Record': The Art of Jazz and the Recording Industry," *The Source: Challenging Jazz Criticism* 2 (March 2005), 63–70.

Derrida, J. [trans. Alan Bass], *Positions*, London: Continuum Press, 2010.

DeVeaux, S., "Constructing the Jazz Tradition: Jazz Historiography," *Black American Literature Forum* 25:3 (Autumn 1991), 525–560.

DeVeaux, S., "Core and Boundaries," *The Source: Challenging Jazz Criticism* 2 (March 2005), 15–30.

DeVito, C. (ed.), *Coltrane on Coltrane: The John Coltrane Interviews*, Chicago, IL: A Cappella Books, 2010.

DeVito, C., Fujioka, Y., Schmaler, W., and Wild., D., *The John Coltrane Reference*, Abingdon, UK, and New York: Routledge, 2008.

Durkheim, E. [trans. Carol Cosman], *The Elementary Forms of Religious Life*, New York: Oxford University Press Worlds Classics, 2008.

Dyer, R., *Heavenly Bodies: Film Stars and Society*, Hampshire: Palgrave Macmillan, 1987.

Dyer, R., *Stars*, London: BFI, 1998.

Eckstein, L., "A Love Supreme: Jazzthetic Strategies in Toni Morrison's *Beloved*," *African American Review* 40.2 (2006), 271–283.

Eisenberg, E., *The Recording Angel: Music, Records and Culture from Aristotle to Zappa*, 2nd ed., New Haven, CT: Yale University Press, 2005.

Elie, L. E., "An Interview with Wynton Marsalis," *Callaloo* 13.2 (Spring 1990), 271–290.

Feld, S., *Jazz Cosmopolitanism in Accra: Five Musical Years in Ghana*, Durham and London: Duke University Press, 2012.

Fraim, J., *Spirit Catcher: The Life and Art of John Coltrane*, West Liberty, OH: Greathouse Company, 1996.

Gabbard, K., "How Many Miles? Alternate Takes on the Jazz Life," in Lock, G., and Murray, D. (eds.), *Thriving on a Riff: Jazz and Blues Influences in African American Literature and Film*, Oxford and New York: Oxford University Press, 2009, 184–200.

Gabbard, K., *Jammin' at the Margins: Jazz and the American Cinema*, Chicago and London: University of Chicago Press, 1996.

Gabbard, K. (ed.), *Jazz Among the Discourses*, Durham and London: Duke University Press, 1995.

Gabbard, K. (ed.), *Representing Jazz*, Durham and London: Duke University Press, 1995.

Gennari, J., *Blowin' Hot and Cool: Jazz and Its Critics*, Chicago and London: University of Chicago Press, 2006.

Gennari, J., "Jazz Criticism: Its Development and Ideologies," *Black American Literature Forum* 25:3 (Fall 1991), 449–523.

Goehr, L., *The Imaginary Museum of Musical Works: An Essay in the Philosophy of Music*, Oxford and New York: Oxford University Press, 1992.

Gottlieb, R. (ed.), *Reading Jazz: A Gathering of Autobiography, Reportage and Criticism from 1919 to Now*, London: Bloomsbury, 1997.

Grey, D. S., *Acknowledgement: A John Coltrane Legacy*, McLean, VA, IndyPublish, 2001.

Griffiths, P., *Modern Music: A Concise History from Debussy to Boulez*, New York: Thames and Hudson, 1990.

Grime, K., "John Coltrane Talks to Jazz News," in DeVito, C. (ed.), *Coltrane on Coltrane: The John Coltrane Interviews* (Chicago, IL: A Cappella Books, 2010), 119–121.

Hall, J. C., *Mercy, Mercy Me: African-American Culture and the American Sixties*, New York: Oxford University Press, 2001.

Harper, M. S., *Dear John, Dear Coltrane*, Urbana and Chicago: University of Illinois Press, 1985 [1970].

Harper, M. S., "Don't They Speak Jazz," *MELUS* 10.1 (Spring 1983), 3–6.

Hemphill, E., "I Want to Talk About You," *Callaloo* 40 (Summer 1989), 473.

Hopkins, P., *A Love Supreme* [Contending Forces], London, X Press, 1995.

Jarrett, M., *Drifting on a Read: Jazz as a Model for Writing*, Albany: State University of New York Press, 1999.

Jarrett, M., "Four Choruses on the Tropes of Jazz Writing," *American Literary History* 6.2 (Summer 1994), 336–353.

Jones, L. [Amiri Baraka], *Black Music*, New York: Da Capo Press, 1998 [1968].

Jost, E., *Free Jazz*, New York: Da Capo Press, 1994.

Kahn, A., "The House That Trane Built," *JazzTimes* (September 2002), 128–129.

Kahn, A., *The House That Trane Built: The Story of Impulse Records*, London: Granta Books, 2006.

Kahn, A., *A Love Supreme: The Creation of John Coltrane's Classic Album*, London: Granta Books, 2002.

Katz, M., *Capturing Sound: How Technology Changed Music*, Berkeley: University of California Press, 2004.

Kofsky, F., *Black Nationalism and the Revolution in Music*, New York: Pathfinder Press, 1970.

Kofsky, F., *John Coltrane and the Jazz Revolution of the 1960s*, London and New York: Pathfinder Press, 1998.

Lauer, B., "John Coltrane and the Replacement Child Syndrome," *Jazz Research Journal* 3.1 (May 2009), 105–117.

Leavis, F. R., *The Great Tradition*, London: Faber and Faber, 2008.

Leonard, N., *Jazz: Myth and Religion*, New York and Oxford: Oxford University Press, 1987.

Liebman, D., "John Coltrane," *Jazz Research Journal* 2.2 (November 2008), 109–118.

Lock, G., "Trane Talk," *Wire* 86 (April 1991), 42–43.

Lock, G., and Murray, D. (eds.), *The Hearing Eye: Jazz and Blues Influences in African American Visual Art*, New York: Oxford University Press, 2009.

Lock, G., and Murray, D. (eds.), *Thriving on a Riff: Jazz and Blues Influences in African American Literature and Film*, New York: Oxford University Press, 2009.

Martin, R., "An Interview with Michael Harper," *Black American Literature Forum* 24.3 (Autumn 1990), 441–451.

Marsalis, W., with Ward, G. C., *Moving to Higher Ground: How Jazz Can Change Your Life*, New York: Random House, 2008.

McDonald, M. B., "Traning the Nineties, or the Present Relevance of John Coltrane's Music of Theophany and Negation," *African American Review* 29.2 (Summer 1995), 275–282.

Merod, J., "A World Without Whole Notes: The Intellectual Subtext of Spike Lee's Blues," *Boundary 2* 18.2 (Summer 1991), 238–251.

Miller, J. A., "'I Investigate the Sun': Amiri Baraka in the 1980s," *Callaloo* 26 (Winter 1986), 184–192.

Modirzadeh, H., "Aural Archetypes and Cyclic Perspectives in the Work of John Coltrane and Ancient Chinese Music Theory," *Black Music Research Journal* 21:1 (Spring 2001), 75–106.

Monson, I. (ed.), *The African Diaspora: A Musical Perspective*, New York and London: Routledge, 2000.

Moore, S., "I Suspect Blue Labour Is Just Another Great Moving-Right Show," *Guardian*, June 25, 2011, p. 36.

Morris, P. (ed.), *The Bakhtin Reader: Selected Writing of Bakhtin, Medvedev and Voloshinov*, London: Edward Arnold, 1994.

Moten, F., *In the Break: The Aesthetics of the Black Radical Tradition*, Minneapolis and London: University of Minnesota Press, 2003.

Murray, A., *From the Briarpatch File: On Context, Procedure, and American Identity*, New York: Pantheon Books, 2001.

Murray, A., *The Omni-Americans: New Perspectives on Black Experience and American Culture*, New York: Outerbridge & Dienstfrey, 1970.

Murray, A., *Stomping the Blues*, London: Quartet Books, 1978.

Newton, F., *The Jazz Scene*, London: Penguin, 1961.

Nicholls, T., "Dominant Positions: John Coltrane, Michel Foucault, and the Politics of Representation," *Critical Studies in Improvisation / Études critiques en improvisation* 2.1 (2006), 1–13.

Nisenson, E., *Ascension: John Coltrane and His Quest*, New York: Da Capo Press, 1995.

Nussey, K., *A Love Supreme: A Novel*, Toronto: Mansfield Press, 2003.

Panish, J., *The Color of Jazz: Race and Representation in Postwar American Culture*, Jackson: University of Mississippi Press, 1997.

Parent, E., and Tosser, G., "The Dilemmas of African-American Orientalism: Coltrane and the Hispanic Imaginary in 'Ole,'" *Jazz Research Journal* 3.1 (May 2009), 63–85.

Parisi, P., *Coltrane*, London: Jonathan Cape, 2012.

Piekut, B., "Race, Community, and Conflict in the Jazz Composers Guild," *Jazz Perspectives* 3.3 (December 2009), 191–231.

Porter, E., *What Is This Thing Called Jazz? African American Musicians as Artists, Critics and Activists*, Berkeley: University of California Press, 2002.

Porter, L., *John Coltrane: His Life and Music*, Ann Arbor: University of Michigan Press, 1998.

Porter, L., "John Coltrane's 'A Love Supreme': Jazz Improvisation as Composition," *Journal of the American Musicological Society* 38.3 (Autumn 1985), 593–621.

Porter, L., DeVito, C., Wild., D., Fujioka, Y., Schmaler, W. (eds.), *The John Coltrane Reference*, New York: Routledge, 2007.

Priestley, B., *John Coltrane*, London: Apollo Press, 1987.

Radano, R., *Lying Up a Nation: Race and Black Music*, Chicago and London: University of Chicago Press, 2003.

Rasula, J., "The Media of Memory: The Seductive Menace of Records in Jazz History," in Gabbard, K. (ed.), *Jazz Among the Discourses*, Durham and London: Duke University Press, 1995, 134–164.

Ratliff, B., *Coltrane: The Story of a Sound*, London and New York: Faber and Faber, 2007.

Rustin, N. (ed.), *Big Ears: Listening for Gender in Jazz Studies*, Durham and London: Duke University Press, 2008.

Ruyter, M. D., "Interview with John Coltrane," in DeVito, C. (ed.), *Coltrane on Coltrane: The John Coltrane Interviews*, Chicago, IL: A Cappella Books, 2010, 247–253.

Saul, S., *Freedom Is, Freedom Ain't: Jazz and the Making of the Sixties*, Cambridge, MA: Harvard University Press, 2003.

Sautman, F. C., "Hip-Hop/Scotch: 'Sounding Francophone' in French and United States Cultures," *Yale French Studies* [France/USA: The Cultural Wars] 100 (2001), 119–144.

Selfridge, J., *John Coltrane: A Sound Supreme*, Danbury, CT: Franklin Watts, 1999.

Shoemaker, B., "Cleaning the Mirror," *Downbeat* (July 1992), 26–29.

Simpkins, C. O., *Coltrane: A Biography*, Perth Amboy, NJ: Herndon House, 1975.

Small, C., *Musicking: The Meanings of Performance and Listening*, Middletown, CT: Wesleyan University Press, 1998.

Smith, M., *John Coltrane: Jazz, Racism and Resistance* [reprint], London: Redwords, 2006.

Storey, J., *Cultural Theory and Popular Culture: An Introduction*, Harlow: Prentice Hall, 2006.

Such, D. G., *Avant-Garde Jazz Musicians Performing "Out There,"* Iowa City: University of Iowa Press, 1993.

Sudhalter, R., *Lost Chords: White Musicians and Their Contribution to Jazz*, New York: Oxford University Press, 1999.

Taylor, A., *Notes and Tones: Musician-to-Musician Interviews*, 2nd ed., New York: Da Capo Press, 1993.

Thiele, B., with Golden, B., *What A Wonderful World: A Lifetime of Recordings*, New York and Oxford: Oxford University Press, 1995.

Thomas, J. C., *Chasin' the Trane: The Music and Mystique of John Coltrane*, New York: Da Capo Press, 1975.

Thomas, L., "Ascension: Music and the Black Arts Movement," in Gabbard, K. (ed.), *Jazz Among the Discourses*, Durham and London: Duke University Press, 1995, 256–274.

Townsend, P., *Jazz in American Culture*, Edinburgh: Edinburgh University Press, 2000.

Tucker, B., "Prejudice Lives: Toward a Philosophy of Black Music Biography," *Black Music Research Journal* 4 (1984), 1–21.

Tucker, S., *Swing Shift: "All Girl" Bands of the 1940s*, Durham and London: Duke University Press, 2000.

Wallenstein, B., "Poetry and Jazz: A Twentieth-Century Wedding," *Black American Literature Forum* [Literature of Jazz Issue] 25.3 (Autumn 1991), 595–620.

Walser, R. (ed.), *Keeping Time: Readings in Jazz History*, Oxford and New York: Oxford University Press, 1999.

Walser, R., "Out of Notes: Signification, Interpretation and the Problem of Miles Davis," *Musical Quarterly* 77.2 (Summer 1993), 343–365.

Watrous, P., "John Coltrane: A Life Supreme," in Woideck, C. (ed.), *The John Coltrane Companion*, London and New York: Omnibus Press, 1998, 56–57.

Watson, P., "Out of This World," *Wire* 86 (April 1991), 34.

Weatherly, T., and Wilentz, T. (eds.), *Natural Process: An Anthology of New Black Poetry*, New York: Hill and Wang, 1970.

Weber, M., *The Protestant Ethic and the Spirit of Capitalism*, New York: Dover, 2003 [1958].

Weinstein, N. C., *A Night in Tunisia: Imaginings of Africa in Jazz*, London: Scarecrow Press, 1992.

Weston, R., and Jenkins, W., *African Rhythms: The Autobiography of Randy Weston*, Durham: Duke University Press, 2010.

Whyton, T., "Four for Trane: Jazz and the Disembodied Voice," *Jazz Perspectives* 1.2 (October 2007), 115–132.

Whyton, T., *Jazz Icons: Heroes, Myths and the Jazz Tradition*, Cambridge: Cambridge University Press, 2010.

Williams, M., *The Jazz Tradition*, Oxford and New York: Oxford University Press, 1983.

Wilmer, V., *As Serious as Your Life: John Coltrane and Beyond*, London: Serpent's Tail, 1992.

Woideck, C., *The John Coltrane Companion: Five Decades of Commentary*, London: Omnibus Press, 1998.

Wolff, J., "The Ideology of Autonomous Art," in Leppert, R., and McClary, S. (eds.), *Music and Society: The Politics of Composition, Performance and Reception*, Cambridge, Cambridge University Press, 1989, 1–12.

Wolff, J., *The Social Production of Art*, 2nd ed., London: Macmillan, 1993.

INDEX

Note: Titles of works are filed under authors/artists, except for those by John Coltrane, which are entered individually. The letter n following a page number refers to an endnote. Illustrations are shown as page numbers in italics.

art 113
artists: fetishization of 37, 38
Ascension 49, 72, 75–86
    compared with *A Love Supreme* 75
    compared with Coleman's *Free Jazz*
        76–7
    and musical convention 78
    nonhierarchical nature of 79–82
    and politics 84
    spiritual themes in 82, 85–6
Atkins, E. Taylor 13
Auslander, Philip: *Performance in a*
    Mediatized World 58
Austerlitz, Paul 110
Averty, Jean-Christophe 36
Ayler, Albert 50, 85

BBC 10
Bach, J. S.: *Art of Fugue* 137n10
Bakhtin, Mikhail 129
Ballads 51
Balliett, Whitney 83
Baraka, Amiri 72–3, 83, 95, 103
    "Jazz and the White Critic" 73
Benston, Kimberley: *Performing Blackness:*
    Enactments of African-American
    Modernism 107, 109, 110
Bergman, Jill 130–1
Berliner, Paul 24
    Thinking in Jazz: the Infinite Art of
    Improvisation 61–2
binaries
    A Love Supreme 14, 15, 21–2, 40
    Derrida, Jacques on 27
    drugs-divine 28, 31
    jazz discourse 11, 12, 13, 27, 39–40
    recorded/live sound 31–5, 58
Black Arts Movement 78, 84, 90, 103
Black Arts Repertory Theater and School 84
black culture 12–13, 72 *see also* African
    American music
black music *see* African American music
blackness 96
Blakey, Art 82
Bley, Carla 135n15
Blue Note 54, 139n28
"Blue Train" 103
blues 72
Bono 117
Brown, James 73

Brown, Leonard: *John Coltrane & Black*
    America's Quest for Freedom 12,
    104, 134n8
Brown, Marion 61, 80, 84

Classic Quartet 70, 105
    A Love Supreme recording session 24–5,
    48, 70, 126
    and advertising 118
    Antibes Juan les Pins Festival (1965) 14,
    32–5, 51
    and *Ascension* 75
    demise of 81
    see also Davis, Art; Garrison, Jimmy;
    Jones, Elvin; Shepp, Archie;
    Tyner, McCoy
Cole, Bill 64
    John Coltrane 103
Coleman, Ornette 72
    Free Jazz 76
Coltrane, Alice 22–3, 24, 59, 93
    interview with Branford Marsalis 25–6
    World Galaxy 105
Coltrane, John 54, 55, 127
    and African American tradition 63, 65,
    73, 104, 107–8, 110, 115, 120–3,
    124, 129
    and African tradition 91, 94, 95, 120–3
    at Antibes Juan les Pins Festival
    (1965) 32–4, 34, 35
    and avant-garde 95
    Baraka, Amiri on 72
    and black consciousness 69
    death of 50, 102, 107
    deification of 59–68, 89
    collaboration with Dolphy, Eric
    138n23
    and drug use 28–31, 49, 79
    and experimentation 46–7
    formative experiences 46
    genius of 18
    human nature of 67–8
    icon of 65, 66
    impact of 62
    and improvisation 87
    and Impulse records 52, 53
    influences on 12, 91
    interviews by 134n8
    with John Coltrane Sextet 92
    legacy of 13, 50, 66–7